33   5—

D0824666

Endurance Riding

The author and Magnet Regent, her Standardbred mare, here shown at the finish of a 100-mile ride in Asheville, North Carolina.

Endurance Riding

Ann Hyland

J. B. LIPPINCOTT COMPANY
Philadelphia & New York

A different version of this book has been
published in England under the title
Beginner's Guide to Endurance Riding
and is © 1974 by Ann Hyland.

U.S. Library of Congress Cataloging in Publication Data

Hyland, Ann.
    Endurance riding.

    Published in London in 1974 under title: Beginner's
guide to endurance riding.
    Includes index.
    1. Endurance riding (Horsemanship)
SF309.H87   1975   798'.23   75–17774
ISBN–0–397–01082–6

To the memory of my father,
Laurence Ross

Contents

A section of photographs follows page 96.

Acknowledgments

I should like to thank the following for their help to me as I compiled this book: R. G. Orton, M.R.C.V.S., adviser to the Endurance Horse and Pony Society in England, who helped with veterinary information; Harold Parr (Associate Farriery Company of London), who gave advice on shoeing; Colin Knapp, who assisted with the tack chapter; Alan Exley and *Horse World* magazine for permission to use portions of published articles I have written on endurance riding.

For their help in providing information on American long-distance rides, I should like to thank Mrs. Lucille Kenyon; Mrs. Wingate Mackay-Smith; Mrs. Drucilla Barner, Secretary to the Western States Trail Ride, Inc.; Mrs. Joan Throgmorton, Secretary to the North American Trail Ride Conference.

For the use of photographs appearing in the book, my thanks to R. P. Nicholson, who provided the sixteen pictures shown on the first seven pages of the photograph section; to Dr. Robert Marshall, for shots taken on the Golden Horseshoe Ride; to A. J. Langstaff, for the photograph taken on Hampshire's 50 Mile Endurance Ride; to Mrs. Lucille Kenyon, for the photograph of herself and Pazzam; to Mrs. Wingate Mackay-Smith, for the photograph of Dr. Matthew Mackay-Smith and Sorya; to Donna Fitzgerald, for the photograph of herself and Witezarif; to Charles E. Barieau, for the photograph of Wendell T. Robie and Nugget; and to William A. V. Cecil, for the frontispiece photograph.

A. H.

Introduction

COMPETITIVE trail riding and endurance riding are closely connected activities that are relative newcomers among equestrian sports, but they are rapidly gaining in popularity as riders realize they do not need a highly bred or expensive show horse to compete. Success is primarily measured by a rider's ability to produce a horse fit enough to tackle a fair and testing course, bringing him across the finish line in good enough condition to turn around and continue on without any danger of his being either physically or mentally overtaxed.

For this the horse needs careful preparation over a lengthy period. Endurance riding offers the opportunity for a tremendous sense of personal achievement, since all training should be done by the person planning to ride the horse competitively. Although there will be some expenses involved with competing, these compare very favorably with other competitions, for this is a down-to-earth sport with no frills, such as special clothes and tack needed for the show horse or an expensive set of jumps for the jumper.

A horse's training can be adapted to nearby terrain, thus incurring no extra expense. The rider may, of course, choose to make trips away from home ground as a part of the training, but these are not absolutely essential. During a season there will be only a fixed number of rides a horse should compete in, so costs of entry fees, away-from-home stabling, and trucking are very much lower than they are in other equestrian sports.

The competitions are attractive because they are run over different parts of the country, offering a welcome change of scene to both horse and rider. Although they are competitive, the main object is to finish the course. Placings or scaled awards are of secondary importance, and the tensions of showing or jumping are almost entirely absent. This makes for a very friendly and informal atmosphere among competitors, who usually look upon rides as opportunities to meet friends made over preceding seasons. Newcomers are given the chance to enter an entirely new world of equine competition where old hands are always ready with encouragement and practical advice and help if needed. It is very difficult to remain tense over a lengthy course, and once en route, riders relax and settle down to the enjoyment of a powerful, rhythmically striding horse, constantly changing scenery, and the companionship of fellow enthusiasts.

Judging of equine events always gives rise to speculation on the winner's merits and the preferences of the judges. Inevitably, competitors' disappointments are often blamed on inadequacy, bias, or ignorance of the judges—charges that are usually unfounded and sour grapes, but there all the same. In competitive trail riding and endurance riding I feel there is the fairest system of arriving at decisions of all equine sports. They are judged purely on the basis of each individual horse's fitness and ability to cover ground at a fair, required speed, and the "judging" is really no more than an analysis of each horse's veterinary score sheet. There is absolutely no preference as to breed, conformation, action, or manners. Everything revolves around the horse's ability to perform regardless of other such criteria. These are relevant only in that the horse best suited to the job inevitably has a higher success rate than his cousin hampered by deficiencies in build or gait.

This book sets out a broad outline of how to go about involving oneself in this expanding sport. It is based on experiences I have had in choosing, training, and riding a variety of horses in both America and Great Britain. This has meant much hard work; some good luck in having the right horse in Magnet Regent, a bay Standardbred mare, right at the beginning when I first became interested in the sport in North Carolina; some disappointments along the route; plus many very happy and rewarding experiences. I hope the knowledge gained from these will help others start out in the satisfying world of competitive trail and/or endurance riding.

The chapters that follow are intended as a guide to the beginner. When you have had experience of your own, you will no doubt develop your own format and methods of training and competing in the many rides opening up in North America today.

Development of the Sport

ALTHOUGH fairly new as a competitive sport, endurance riding has a very old history, for it was mainly owing to the horse that successive civilizations were able to spread over the world instead of remaining in isolated pockets. It was on the horse's back that conquering armies rode, impressing their mode of life on subjugated peoples and assimilating many of their customs.

In ancient days—the days of the Assyrians, Hittites, Persians, Greeks, and Romans, all of whom had very effective cavalry—the unflagging war horse was essential to carving out empires. Armies rode many, many hundreds of miles. In several cases—Alexander the Great, Xenophon's Retreat of the Ten Thousand, and the Mongol Hordes come to mind—distances were measured in the several thousand miles. Throughout these epic maneuvers both men and horses endured extremes of climate, hunger, and fatigue as well as the dangers of war. Even the legendary Pony Express, with its drain on horse- and manpower, was anticipated by twenty-five hundred years in the time of Darius the Great, whose network of post roads covered his vast dominions. The Susa-to-Sardis run of over 1500 miles was ridden in the extraordinary time of six days.

Later the Huns, and then the Mongols, rode out of the East to infiltrate and conquer the West. Their horse herds numbered in the hundreds of thousands and the distances they traveled attained epic proportions. Arabian horses carried Islam's warriors on their conquering path, especially into Spain, where their legacy of breed and style of riding can still be seen in the modern horse and horseman. Charlemagne's cavalry was instrumental in welding many small states into the first cohesive Christian empire.

In modern times, too, nations' cavalries had set the standards for endurance riding; many of today's competitive rides are based on the old-time marches that were part and parcel of army life. My own farrier recalls one such endurance march in the early 1930s, when he was a member of the 14/20th King's Hussars regiment stationed in Egypt. Each troop was given three days to make a 90-mile trek out of Cairo across shifting desert sands, and take at the end a twenty-four-hour break. Then the real test began—the 90-mile return trip, which had to be accomplished in twelve hours. They set out at 4 P.M. and were back at the Pyramids at 4 A.M. Each horse carried over 300 pounds and proceeded at walk, trot, and canter for five-minute intervals, repeated throughout the ride. In my farrier's particular troop, thanks to very sound animal management, there was no attrition.

In 1920, 1921, and 1922, the Arab Horse Society of Great Britain held 300-mile five-day rides, and just prior to the last war, from 1937 on, *Country Life* and *Riding* magazines held 100-mile-in-three-days rides which were enthusiastically received by British horsemen.

In the United States this sport is very well established today. There are many annual rides, and a tremendous amount of research has been done in the field of care, training, veterinary attention, and all aspects of endurance horse management, especially by those well-known endurance riders Linda Tellington Jones and Wentworth Tellington.

The American rides are split into two broad categories: endurance rides of 50 to 100 miles in one day, the winner being the fastest fit, sound horse; and competitive trail rides, again varying from 25 to 100 miles and from one to three days' duration, the winner in this case being the horse with the highest veterinary score. The most notable is the world-famous Tevis Cup 100 Miles One Day Ride, run in late July or early August from Tahoe City to Auburn, California. Traveling a trail that crosses the Sierra Nevada—exceptional testing ground with steep gradients and tough going—the winner invariably finishes in a ridden time of well under thirteen hours. The 100-mile one-day rides are increasing in popularity, each year bringing new additions to endurance riders' calendars.

On the East Coast the 100-mile-in-three-days competitive rides start with the Florida ride in March, followed by rides throughout spring, summer, and autumn in most eastern seaboard states, including Virginia, New Jersey, Vermont, Maine, and North Carolina. They are based on the old army 300-mile rides and judging is on the basis of time and condition.

In Australia endurance riding has been a thriving sport since 1966, when the Quilty 100 Mile Ride was first staged. The Quilty—named for a colorful Australian stockman who donated a solid gold cup as the trophy—has become famous as a world classic. It is run over a steep, difficult course in New South Wales' Blue Mountains, in climatic conditions that vary from warm to hot, with humidity sometimes very high—all taking a toll of horses and riders. People of many nations, including top endurance riders of Tevis Cup fame—such as Pat and Donna Fitzgerald and Marion Robie—come to compete.

The judging criteria in the Quilty and other Australian endurance rides are that a horse must arrive at the veterinary checks in reasonable condition, and that within thirty minutes thereafter his pulse must be back to 70—difficult after severe stress in some of the toughest country in the world. No horse is allowed out with a higher pulse rate; physical injuries also result in elimination.

The first Quilty was won by Shalawi, an Arabian stallion that has since had a 50-miler named in his honor. Since 1966 several 50- and 75-milers have become part of the yearly Australian equine performance scene. Rules for competing have been based largely upon those of American rides, since the United States has been the modern pioneer with an accumulation of specific knowledge behind its broad scope of competitive rides.

In Britain the current surge of interest dates from 1965. After a long period of inactivity in this field, the Arab Horse Society again ventured into endurance riding with the help of London's *Daily Telegraph*, staging the first Golden Horseshoe ride on Exmoor, a large tract of rough moorland in the south-west of England, with a 50-mile course. Successive years have seen a tightening of the rules and a lengthening of the course so that nowadays the Golden Horseshoe is 75 miles and the courses are selected with great attention paid to testing conditions. To gain a Golden Horseshoe today, horses must be considerably fitter and travel much faster than originally required, averaging a minimum of 9 mph unless severity of going dictates a lowering of the speed in special circumstances. The annual Golden Horseshoe Ride is now run jointly by the Arab Horse Society and the British Horse Society and is among the high spots in British endurance riders' calendars, prefaced by a variety of shorter qualifying rides throughout spring and summer.

Early in 1973 the Endurance Horse and Pony Society (EHPS) was formed to cater specifically to British long-distance-ride enthusiasts. It has modeled its aims and rulings on the well-tried and successful format of the American 100-mile competitive rides, modifying its rules in accordance with British conditions. Two highly competitive rides and several pleasure rides were held in its first year, and a full schedule of events now provides the quickly growing membership with a wide choice of competitive rides. With its stated aim of stimulating the breeding, conditioning, and use of good saddle horses in long-distance rides, the Society is promoting keen interest in the sport and has recently established its first 100-mile-in-24-hours ride, based on the successful format of the Tevis Cup.

With knowledge gained from both Golden Horseshoe rides and EHPS events a considerable range of statistics is being built up in Britain, augmented by American data. Now that Britains, Americans, Australians, and West Germans as well are among the ranks of long-distance riders, endurance riding can look forward to healthy growth. It may well ultimately become an established international competitive sport with the different countries' experiences being pooled for the greater benefit of all.

Choosing the Endurance Horse

ONCE you have decided that endurance riding and/or competitive trail riding appeals to you, the first step is to choose your competitive horse.

In general, any sound, fit horse should be capable of performing creditably on long-distance rides which are run at approximately 6 to 7 mph, and over distances of between 25 and 40 miles to be covered in one day. Under 25 miles, stress symptoms with a fit horse rarely show, and between 25 and 40 miles, the stresses should only be sufficient to sort the very fit from the fit, without any damaging effects to the horses.

It is when you are contemplating more demanding involvement that selection of your horse becomes important. Competing in a 100-miler run over three days, where the 40 miles is repeated on the second day, followed by the final 20 on the third day, means that choosing the right horse could make the difference between a completion award and dropping out en route because of stress, fatigue, or one of the many forms of lameness brought on by the testing 100 miles of travel. You need to be even more selective when choosing the right mount for a ride incorporating both higher speeds and extended distances to be covered in one day, such as the 50- and 100-milers in the American rides and the Golden Horseshoe and Endurance Horse and Pony Society rides in Britain. There are three possible means of obtaining the right horse: selecting and buying him; using one you already have which seems a likely candidate; or—if you have the enthusiasm, foresight, and patience to wait—raising a horse that you have either bred or purchased as a foal bred from proven stock.

Before considering specific breeds, it is important to define the qualities that are especially necessary to developing winning endurance performance. These have to do with three considerations: conformation, temperament, and gaits.

Conformation

The ideal endurance horse should be fairly small—around 15 hands, give or take an inch or so. He should be very compact, for compactness indicates greater strength than the strung-out horse with an exceptionally long back and the frequently accompanying weak loin area.

He should be deep through the heart, with a well-developed chest affording ample lung room. The rib cage should be generous and the loins strong; shoulder, pasterns, and hooves should slope as close as possible to 45 degrees for a smooth ride and minimal leg concussion. Pasterns should be neither too short, which could result in a jarring ride and leg concussion, nor disproportionately long, which often means inherent weakness. Throatlatch should be wide and clean, giving good wind passage; hooves should have good quality horn, as dry, split-prone hooves cannot hold shoes nearly as well and lack resilience. Heels should be wide, not pinched in, and the frogs healthy so they can do their special job of shock absorbing. (The all-important subject of hooves and shoeing is discussed separately and fully in the next chapter.)

Quarters should be strong and muscular because from this section of the horse comes the driving power essential to effortless, rhythmic stride; legs should be of good, strong bone, with muscular forearms, large flat knees, and short, strong cannon bones, with the tendons clearly defined and not fleshy, which could indicate weakness. Hocks should be well let down, again giving short cannon bones behind. Look for straight hocks, not hocks carried too far under or too close together, as both conditions could well involve weakness and result in too much strain over a grueling course. Hocks too close together may mean the horse could interfere in his action behind.

Many of the more substantial types of riding horses have

infusions of drafthorse blood and, although undoubtedly weight carriers, they are not ideal mounts for endurance work unless crossed with a lighter breed. Avoid any horse with too coarse a conformation; heavy, rounded bone (not to be confused with good dense bone); heavy, ploddy, or choppy gaits. These types will tire easily, wearying both themselves and their riders, and a tired rider tends to ride heavily, which in turn results in back problems for the horse.

While on the subject of bone, I must also say something about the physical condition carried. There are three basic types: the heavy-boned horse carrying gross flesh; the middle-of-the-road type carrying sufficient condition, which, even when out of work, does not run to fat; and the greyhound type that, try as you may, you cannot induce to carry any appreciable condition. The middle-of-the-road type is preferable, as he has a reserve of condition without carrying too much bulk of bone, fat, and muscle in the first place, which puts excessive strain on heart, wind, and limbs. The greyhound variety often goes with a fretful disposition or unsuitable conformation.

While checking conformation, do not forget to make sure the horse's teeth are in good condition and that the bite enables him to chew his food properly, as a horse getting less than the best from his rations will not carry the condition necessary for the work demanded of him. Regular veterinary attention is necessary if the teeth are suspect; floating (filing) can improve their efficiency. Grain being passed in any appreciable quantity is a warning sign that teeth need attention.

Temperament

Look first for a large, expressive eye; it will give you a pretty good initial lead to the horse's temperament, which should be generous, lively, but amenable. Frequently horses with other than ideal temperaments do perform superbly, but how much better to have your endurance horse's moods dovetailing with your own. With endurance riding, where so many hours are spent working together, the bond between horse and rider can become a true fusion of effort and will.

My own ideal is a horse that is itching to give a lot more than is asked for but is mannerly enough to accept restraint without fretting, which wastes precious physical energy. I have been very fortunate in owning several such horses both in the past and currently. In America I had an Arabian stallion, Royal Command, of Al-Marah breeding, and a Standardbred mare, Magnet Regent, by Prince Regent out of Red Magic. I still have the Standardbred in England. In addition I also have another American-bred Arabian stallion, Nizzolan, by Lewisfield Nizzamo out of Solange (the Nizzam line has also produced Pazzam, Lucille Kenyon's great 100-miler), and a grade paint pony who, although a little smaller than the ideal, makes up for it in larger-than-pony performance with an exceptionally good strong nonponyish stride and generous nature. All these horses have this keenness allied with sensible natures, plus the vital reserve and prompt acceleration often demanded from endurance horses. The future for me is in the shape of Zoltan, a two-year-old colt by Nizzolan out of my Standardbred mare Magnet Regent.

Another aspect of the horse's temperament relates to the condition he should carry. I once had a mare for whom I entertained great hopes. She was fast, inexhaustible, clean-legged, and great-hearted. In fact she was everything a good endurance horse should be, with one exception. This became apparent when I took her to a show that meant two nights away from home. She refused to eat—in fact, she sulked the whole time. One-day shows were fun, but not when it meant living in strange quarters. Hence I reevaluated her, realizing that a fretting horse that wouldn't eat was hardly suitable for endurance riding. I couldn't afford chancing a horse working on its nerves, losing condition, and running up light.

Gaits

Gaits are inseparably allied to conformation. Good gaits usually go with good conformation, and if these are combined with the right disposition, the result should be an excellent prospect.

Endurance horses should possess a long, free, elastic stride and be equally comfortable on both diagonals at the trot and leads at the canter for minimal fatigue to both rider and horse. Horses with the right conformation and basically good strides at all gaits can be schooled to use themselves to maximum effect with minimum effort. Some irregularities, particularly wrong leads, can be traced to a horse who is stiffer on one side, and most horses do have one side more supple than the other, bending and picking up leads better on that side. Proper schooling is called for in both cases.

At the trot some horses are more comfortable on one diagonal than the other. There are three possible reasons for this. The rider may always use the same diagonal, usually unwittingly; or the horse may habitually switch the rider to his preferred one; or the horse may favor one diagonal because of faulty hoof trimming. This last was proved—and solved—for me in Florida with my Standardbred. Bill Tobin, the farrier, took one look at her hooves and brought out his hoof leveler. He found the angle of one hoof was 5 degrees different from the angle of the other. He corrected the hoof and the problem corrected itself. If you suspect a trusted farrier has erred in this respect, approach him tactfully about it; good, qualified farriers are always at a premium.

Any irregularity in a horse's gait could be tiring to him, putting him under undue strain. Although most horses will learn to compensate adequately for the irregularity, it is best to have a mount free of them. Not to be confused with irregularities that hinder—for example, hitching or winging—are the gaits that are perfectly normal in one horse, yet abnormal in another. I again illustrate this point with my Standardbred, who, when she extends at the trot, brings her hind hooves out and to the side, extending the stride a couple of feet beyond those of other breeds. This gives an advantageously long stride with a very wide track behind, and by such width she avoids any possibility of overreach. This is normal to her breed when speed is called for, but in others it could prove very tiring. Arabians also frequently have a very wide track behind when in a powerful driving trot.

Horses that have a tendency to overreach, forge, brush, knock themselves, and so forth, should be avoided if at all possible as the gamble is too great and the disappointments too bitter. It could even be that a horse knocks himself and is momentarily lame, and if that moment comes at an inopportune time, lost points or even withdrawal from the ride may result.

A horse with these tendencies, even when fit, is in danger of damaging himself when he is pushed and under strain at consistent high speed. Many interferences occur when a horse is beginning to tire, so don't select a horse that interferes before he even starts the course.

Two points to bear in mind regarding various interferences. Some ride rules do not permit any protective equipment to be used; the premise is that a horse needing these is not a true endurance horse. Other rides do permit protective boots and such. Nevertheless, over a period of time and under track conditions these create their own problems; if a chafe results, your horse may develop abrasions from mud and grit lodged between boot and skin. He will then be penalized on points, or, if the galling is severe enough, eliminated altogether.

To repeat: choosing the ideal horse means searching for one that combines good conformation, strong striding gaits, and a generous but sensible temperament.

Consideration of all these points is, of course, also relevant if you decide to breed your own future mount. For this—although there is always a very strong element of chance in any breeding program since even the best mare put to the best stallion does not always produce highly competent offspring— the chances are more than very good that the results gained by selective breeding will produce a future winner. A young foal with the right breeding can be purchased, or if you have either a suitable mare or, in some cases, both mare and stallion, the right crossing will give a youngster with unlimited potential. The raising and conditioning of the youngster will be in your own hands. Particularly if you intend the foal as a future endurance prospect, feed him exceptionally well in his early years. It will pay high dividends later in his working life. Also do have his hooves attended to by a competent farrier right from foalhood; remember those hooves will be carrying him over thousands of miles in later competitions and training buildups.

Many horses are subjected to work too young. Some, although appearing in top condition at time of purchase, may have had a bad patch in growth or in feeding levels sometime in their younger formative years that the prospective owner knows nothing about. Also disposition may have some undesirable quirks not immediately apparent. With breeding your own, most of these pitfalls can be avoided.

The most likely starting point will be the mare owner who is going to raise a foal with endurance riding as the long-term goal, particularly if the owner already has a suitable mount and needs a youngster coming on. Decide if the mare possesses at least the majority of the points already outlined, particularly in regard to conformation and disposition. Once having satisfied yourself she has, send her, if possible, to a stallion that has already proved himself in competitive trail and/or endurance riding by gaining the highest awards available in whichever sphere he competes in. Particularly with the 100-mile-in-three-days competitive trail rides, the placings and awards can be a little misleading because loss of veterinary points can stem from several sources, and this loss reflects on the horse's overall score and ride placing. Occasionally loss of veterinary points has nothing whatsoever to do with a horse's own capacity to endure stress, but may have been occasioned by ill-fitting tack which raised pressure bumps; or the same condition might have been caused by a bad rider sitting incorrectly, thus creating chafing or bruising around tack areas. The judges on a ride are there to adjudicate on what they see before them, not to have excuses presented by the rider for various minor faults that arise. So when considering a horse that has lost veterinary marks, find out if they were caused by horse or by rider failure—that is, by the horse's reaction to stress or by the rider himself.

If the sire you are considering has no proven endurance record, find out his history in performance events that demand a consistently high output of energy and also subject the horse to considerable stress. If he has a performance record in which physical breakdowns, as opposed to injuries, have been entirely absent, go ahead and use him. If the stallion has no specific performance record, ask about his progeny or close relatives. These angles should give you a pretty good idea of the type of foal which will result, particularly if your mare has already proved herself adequate in performance. However, it is unusual to find stallions standing at stud that have done nothing whatsoever, as most owners do campaign them in one way or another.

Above all, avoid breeding from any stock that has broken down under stress or gone lame through inherent weakness. Such horses may be all right for general-purpose riding stock that will never be subjected to heavy stress, but they are not the material to use for producing endurance horses.

The fact that a horse is a show winner does not necessarily mean he will make a good endurance horse. Although conformation may be superb, temperament under ride conditions is not likely to have been tried out because top show horses rarely compete in long-distance rides or other very arduous activities, at least not while they are being show campaigned. The two just don't seem to go together, although it would be gratifying to see a really honest working horse in hard condition come up a show winner; if a horse works well enough to win in hard performance there cannot be anything much wrong with his conformation. However, show temperament and ride temperament might not tally, and temperament does play a tremendous part in successful long-distance riding.

The third choice, most common for those just entering the sport—at least until the sport expands to the point that horse owners breed specifically for it—is to use the horse you already have, provided he meets the necessary temperament and conformation requirements. If those standards are met, it is then absolutely vital, right at the outset of your training program, to overcome any tendency you may have toward stable-blindness and to make an honest assessment of whatever drawbacks and limitations your horse has and then, where possible, to work either to overcome them or to minimize their negative effects. It is essential to be aware of such drawbacks at the outset.

For instance, imagine what damage could be done to a horse with a tendency toward minor leg troubles (such as puffy or slightly strained tendons or ligaments; filling, stocking up, sprains, fever in the limbs through stress) if these were unsuspected, as they could well be if the horse had not previously been worked hard. The harm would be done, possibly irreparably, without the caution bred of foreknowledge. In minor cases correct training can serve to strengthen, whereas injudicious use can be ruinous.

Several gait and hoof irregularities can be helped by corrective shoeing. Minor leg ailments can often be overcome by good veterinary advice, followed by correct treatment and constant awareness of the problem so that no undue risks are taken.

Notes on Specific Breeds

Study of long-distance rides in the United States, Britain, and Australia—the three countries where endurance riding is a healthy, progressive sport—shows the highest percentage of successes has been achieved by horses of either pure or part Arabian blood. In my view, this is not a matter of chance, but an indication that this breed is considered, and proven, to be the best for the work. The Arab has been bred for centuries under what are seen by horsemen as far from ideal raising conditions in that he has had to endure extremes of climate, short rations in both the feed and water departments, and tough going over either sand or sharp rocky footing. Since the Arabian is a horse that was a necessity rather than a luxury to the nomad Bedouin tribes as a conveyance in both war and travel, stamina, courage and speed were the essentials looked for in his makeup. These attributes have combined to produce the endurance horse par excellence, because what he is now asked to do for his rider's pleasure and sport he once did from necessity. The partbred Arabian retains in the cross much of the purebred's toughness and resilience.

I cite a few examples from my own experiences that lead me to favor this breed. During the 1967 Florida 100-miler, where I rode a five-year-old Arab stallion, temperatures rose to between 110 and 120 degrees at one point in a part of the route that seemed to trap the heat. This excessive heat caused many cases of heat founder. My Arab, along with the other Arabians, was unaffected, and at the finish Arabians filled 80 percent of the placings in the lightweight, heavyweight, and junior divisions.

In the Tevis Cup, the acme of endurance riding, where horses travel 100 miles in a day over some of the world's toughest, roughest terrain, Arabians have been the most frequent winners. In fact many of the top horses have remained fit enough to tackle this, and many other very tough rides, on a repeat basis, appearing in the winning and placing slots for several successive seasons.

In Australia, as noted earlier, the first 100-miler was won by Shalawi, an Arabian stallion. In Great Britain each year's lineup of award winners at the Golden Horseshoe ride shows that the "Gold"—currently the top award for endurance horses —is usually won by Arab or part-Arab horses. In the three Golden Horseshoes I have entered since my own stallion, Nizzolan, was old enough to compete, three out of four winners in 1972, five out of seven in 1973, and six out of eleven in 1974 were Arabs or part-Arabs.

Owing to their heritage and selective breeding for performance in their country of origin, Arabians are tough, courageously willing, and innately sensible; they do not waste precious energy in frivolity when really working; they have an exceptionally dense yet fine bone and are relatively free of leg troubles. They can also take tremendous strain with no apparent ill effects. Because of their compact build (they have fewer vertebrae than other breeds) their strength in ratio to their size is outstanding, and they can carry more weight than the same-sized horse of a different breed. I recall one very fit, compact purebred Arabian, approximately 14.2 hands high, successfully carrying 240 pounds (a six-foot-plus rider and stock saddle) in one of the Florida rides.

The notion persists, in Britain especially, that the tall and/or heavy person needs a correspondingly larger and/or heavier horse. Purely from the visual aspect this may be so, but in terms of performance it does not follow. On the whole Americans tend to ride smaller horses. In any case, anyone who is considering the 16-plus hand, heavily built mount should be warned that performance does not come in ratio to size, and that in some instances size may work to the horse's disadvantage. The Arabian, for all his dainty looks, is anything but fragile, combining strength with a weight-carrying capacity not related to his own bulk, with added bonuses of speed and stamina. In countries where horses are still used for work— especially on ranches—smaller, more compact animals are found best suited to the work, since they are both tougher and handier.

Up to now the Arabian has been almost synonymous with high cost, but as the breed is becoming increasingly popular for general riding purposes on both sides of the Atlantic, and the Arab Horse Societies in both countries encourage the gelding of all but the best potential sires, more Arabians are coming onto the market at prices both favorable and comparable to good stock of other breeds.

A wealth of American breeds have been developed over the past couple of centuries which generally produce horses suited to hard work and extended mileage. They include the Morgan, Quarterhorse, Appaloosa, Tennessee Walker, Saddlebred, and Standardbred. This wide selection, plus the availability of worldwide breeds such as the Arabian and Thoroughbred, means that real care should be taken in selection of your endurance mount, and an understanding of each particular breed's capabilities and work tasks should be taken into account. Also over the years the foundation stock of many of the British native breeds has been brought across the Atlantic so that for the smaller, lighter rider there is the added choice of horses resulting from a mountain or moorland pony crossed with one of the larger breeds, usually the Arabian or the Thoroughbred.

Setting aside the purebred Arabian, which in my opinion is the best breed for endurance competition, it is worthwhile to consider the native American breeds, or a crossing of these breeds, one by one.

The Thoroughbred, though having many of the desirable qualities such as courage and good conformation, frequently has a highly strung temperament that tends to burn itself out early. The breed is also prone to leg problems. One must remember that the Thoroughbred on the whole is bred as a superb racing machine which was never intended for the extended grind of endurance work. Thoroughbreds usually tend to be over the ideal height for endurance work, which means that they have to expend part of their energies in transporting this extra size rather than injecting all their energies into covering the miles.

However, crossing a Thoroughbred with one of the previously mentioned British large native ponies such as Connemara or New Forest can produce a really first class endurance mount of around 14.2 to 15 hands which embodies the courage, fire, and speed of the Thoroughbred while retaining the durability and toughness of the native pony. I have seen Connemara and

New Forest crossed with Thoroughbred and Arabian, and both types do produce excellent endurance mounts. Thoroughbred crossed with Quarterhorse or Appaloosa produces a tough mount with the assets of the Thoroughbred and the durability and the handiness of the recognized working ranch horses—handiness that is very important when negotiating tricky footing.

The Standardbred is my first choice after the Arabian, partly because I have had personal experience with this breed, and partly because Standardbreds are subjected to a far more rigorous energy output on the track than Thoroughbreds, and durability is considered in their breeding. The Standardbred, whether a trotter or pacer, does these gaits naturally without artificial training, so there is no added strain in producing his gaits. His conformation, though not show oriented, is robust and also is ideally suited to speed and endurance. In my experience, too, the Standardbred has a more levelheaded disposition than many other breeds, while still maintaining the urge to give his speedy best. One word of caution, however. Avoid the Standardbred that has been to the track. Those tracks are set like cement, and because the horses are raced and trained continually on that footing, many leg ailments occur with Standardbreds in training that would not happen on natural going. Also, those that come out of racing usually do so because of breakdown or a bad track record. Either way their legs have taken a pounding. There are many, however, that never make the grade for racing and have therefore not been subjected to such conditions for any appreciable period. The fact that a Standardbred is not fast enough for the track does not mean he is not a superb horse in other spheres, and such horses could well be ideal for endurance work.

Neither the Saddlebred nor the Tennessee Walker, while initially bred for traveling long distances, is in my estimation the ideal mount for competitive trail and/or endurance work, though many such horses do perform admirably. Like the Thoroughbred, they do tend to be over the average in height, and they have man-induced gaits which tend to take more out of them than the completely natural gaits of other breeds. Granted these gaits after centuries do come easily; they are nevertheless gaits which are encouraged for the ease of man on his horse, not the gaits that take the least out of the mount. Both breeds also tend to be rather highly strung, and the best endurance horses are those that strike a happy balance between the highly strung and the placid animal.

The Quarterhorse and the Appaloosa breeds have both produced some ideal endurance mounts. They generally come within the appropriate size range, and both breeds possess equable temperaments. They have a capacity for hard work because they have been bred primarily for range work. However, if you are selecting a mount from either of these two breeds, bear in mind two possible disadvantages that arise mainly from their build. Since they were originally intended as working cow-horses, part of their daily chores included some of the heavier ranch tasks of roping. For this a stockier, more heavily fleshed and muscled animal was required, and this is not the ideal type for endurance riding. Often too the ride the heavier built animal gives is somewhat jarring, akin to the English cob—superb at his job, but not ideal for a day spent covering many miles at considerable speed. But happily in both these breeds there are horses of lighter build, often produced by a good admixture of Thoroughbred blood, which gives the speed and verve while still retaining the breeds' innate sense and stamina. So in considering either Quarterhorse or Appaloosa, look for the more streamlined horse that does not have an excess of muscle, fat, or bone to hamper him.

Finally, the Morgan. This breed has always shown outstanding vigor and stamina in whatever task it was asked to do, and it combines the right build, the disposition, and the natural gaits for endurance riding. Not as widespread over the country as the breeds previously mentioned, in its own home and neighboring states the Morgan has shown it is admirably suited to the sport.

These notes on breed selection are not meant as a criticism of any breed which in my opinion is not ideal for endurance work, but only to point out that some breeds are generally better suited to it than others. Again and again in the horse world the unexpected comes up a winner, so if you have a horse and want to try him in endurance, assess his capabilities, put him into training, bearing his good points and faults in mind, and go to it.

Finally, when you do put your horse into training, bear in mind his type with regard to distance and speed requirements and do not attempt more than you know he is really capable of. Feel your way into competitive trail riding and endurance riding. Use the first season to learn and experiment. I know I learned a tremendous amount on my first 100-miler in Florida, returning home full of plans for future rides and also wondering whatever made me think before the ride that I knew a fair bit. I found there was a mass of practical knowledge to accumulate. I also found the bunch of riders on that ride the friendliest and most helpful group ever, so different from shows where the competition is so knife-edge keen. It is better to complete a ride successfully than to overdo it trying for a win, only to have to withdraw through some stress failure.

In any case, if you are at all unsure about your horse's suitability, whether a purchased prospect, stock you want to breed from, or a horse you already have, get the advice of your own vet, who will be able to advise on the horse's (or the prospective parents') structural capabilities.

Hooves and Shoeing

"NO hoof, no horse"—an old horseman's saw, very true and descriptive. It is particularly so in the case of the endurance horse because he will be subjected to great stresses and strains, all directly bearing on his hooves.

Race horses, it's true, are subjected to severe strains, as are jumpers, eventers, and polo horses. But all these travel over ground that yields to the hoof, offering no impediments to forward movement beyond the conditions brought on by weather which may affect the going. Furthermore, horses in other competitive sports are allowed added protection of strengthening liniments, supporting bandages, protective boots, and soles of leather or metal between shoe and hoof if any of these are considered necessary. The endurance horse, however, must be prepared to cover absolutely any type of terrain since, to offer a true test of a horse's ability to endure, the course will be set out over as great a variety of ground as ride locality allows. And while some ride rules permit the use of various protective aids, other ride rules, mainly those for competitive trail riding, do not. Check on these points before entering. Necessary care with liniment should be given in plenty of time prior to the rides so that application can be discontinued well ahead of ride day, allowing any lingering traces to disappear. While the need for liniment is only temporary, supports and protective boots both indicate a fault in conformation or way of going and cover up defects which in all probability cannot be cured—another reason to take great care in selecting a horse.

During competitive rides, among the types of ground I have encountered are: sandy firm going; sandy shifting, heavy going with the sand 18 inches deep in places for considerable stretches; slick grass with no bite to it as the undersoil was baked hard; gravelly tracks with small-size stones; tracks constructed almost solely of flints, many of which had sharp edges protruding; slippery shale; rock; heavy mud and sucking clay; freshly turned earth that holds the feet; slippery, hard-paved roads. Happily, my experience has regularly included a rider's dream of good going, where time can be made up that was lost on footing needing careful and slower negotiation. In Britain there is the ubiquitous roadwork with which every British rider has at some time to contend, since there are more saddle horses per capita to less ideal riding ground than in almost any other country. In the United States in some localities riders are similarly hampered, but there are countless miles of open riding country offering marvelous freedom.

From this list of the conditions a rider can expect to meet —if not in one competition, at least during an active competitive year—it is clear that the hoof's construction and care are extremely important. Sandy soil means a wearing aggravation in loose shoes or hoof cracks, with the fine particles of sand working between hoof and shoe or between the edges of a hoof crack, which gradually widens till the split becomes a real problem. Most hoof cracks occur in the first place because proper care was lacking and the overgrown hoof split and broke around its edges. Heavy sand, mud, or clay sucks on the shoe, loosening it if the clenches are risen or if the hoof has grown considerably since the last shoeing. On slick grass a worn shoe with no bite or traction left can upend a horse or cause him to slip badly with resultant strain to either tendons or muscles. Gravel can pinprick a thin sole or work into cracks or between a loose shoe and the hoof. Flints and sharp stones may bruise soles. Shale and roadwork need shoes with a good bite, meaning freshly shod hooves with nail grip.

When you are selecting and conditioning your endurance horse, the first thing to look for is the general structure of the hooves. They should be both deep and wide, without the excessive size that comes under the heading of "dinner-plate feet." Such hooves are usually very shallow in construction.

When you examine the feet, pay particular attention to the underparts of the hoof, as these are abused by the terrain. The sole should be arched or concave, not flat or dropped, which brings it into contact with, or too close to, the ground. If possible, I should like to see my prospective endurance horse's hooves unshod at first, so as to check how he reacts to stony ground. This would also show his true gaits, as shoeing can often alter a horse's way of going. The frog should be resilient and deep and wide at the heel; otherwise it cannot do its job as a shock absorber. The wall of the hoof should be thick, ideal minimum measurements being ¼ inch at the heel increasing to ½ inch at the toe. The angle of the hoof from coronet to ground should ideally be 45 degrees. If it is too sloped, excessive strain will be put on pasterns and limbs, and if too upright, there will be more concussion because the gait will be less springy. The hoof angle is normally repeated in the slope of pastern and shoulder so the workings of hooves, shoulders, and legs are closely interrelated.

Even the best of feet will not remain in good condition unless they receive adequate professional care. While I was living in America I found that it was often difficult to get a good farrier owing to the distances he had to cover. Hence many of the local horsemen had become handy do-it-yourself horseshoers. This was purely a question of putting shoes on the hooves, not selecting the correct shoe for the job. With so much at stake it is worth the added expense and trouble to get the very best farrier you can, and to make a set of regular appointments with him to maintain continuity of care.

A good hoof's efficiency can be impaired and its shape altered to a shallower, too wide construction if the horse is subjected to excessive work while too young, before the hoof has finished growing. Constant pressure will cause too great an expansion, resulting in shallow feet with their accompanying problems.

A healthy, strong hoof will grow between ¼ and ⅝ inch a month. Monthly, or at most six-weekly, intervals between the farrier's visits are necessary, for either new shoes or a reset of the old ones. Neglect of hoof length can cause strains, general breakdown of laminae, and risen clenches, which turn the clench into a cutting hazard standing out from the hoof.

If the hoof is allowed to grow too long, the horse's angle of placement changes. As the toe grows outward and forward more pressure is put on the heel. The old shoe becomes im-bedded in the hoof, causing pressure in the wrong places, espe-cially at the heel, where corns may set in. As new, untended hoof grows, there will be a gradual splitting and weakening of the wall as old hoof separates and grows over and around the shoe. Hooves neglected in winter layoff months may be in bad shape for spring and summer conditioning, thereby hindering action and ability to work to full capacity.

With the normal hoof and normal action, the best shoe for endurance work is the concave fullered type made from stock not less than ⅝ inch wide and not less than ⁷⁄₁₆ inch thick. The fullered shoe offers more grip and, because of the air pocket, makes retraction easier, especially in holding going, resulting in less physical strain on tendons, legs, and body. With less pull on the shoe itself clenches will stay tight longer, minimizing the possibility of thrown shoes.

There are a few points worth mentioning which are applica-ble to the shoeing of any horse. Beware of having the shoes burned on to see if they fit. Repeated burnings will tend to dry the hooves and reduce their resilience. Again, a hoof should not have too many nail holes, as an excessive number tends to weaken the wall. A good farrier can often use the old holes a second time, provided of course the horse's hooves are attended to on a regular basis.

The outer surface of the hoof should not be rasped. Some farriers are inclined to do this as it makes the hoof appear neater, but it should be done only to smooth the tips of the clenches, as it permits the natural oils present in the hoof to dissipate. This is one instance when a hoof preparation can help alleviate the dryness and resultant splitting that can result from overrasping.

Another point to watch for is to make sure that the heels

are not cut so low to the ground that the flexor tendons are subjected to excessive strain. Any change in the hoof angle, such as corrective trimming and shoeing would occasion, should be done gradually, as too sudden a change can strain tendons, causing temporary lameness. The same thing can result from incorrectly fitted studs, which will tend to throw the horse's weight forward onto his toe.

A great number of horses are cold shod all their working lives, but if at all possible try to get a farrier who does hot shoeing. If you employ a farrier who visits your stable, use one who has a portable forge, as many do. The advantages of hot over cold shoeing are that the new shoe can be shaped in the forge to fit any changes in a hoof's growth exactly. Cold shoeing, unless the horse's feet exactly conform to a ready-made size, can only approximate adequacy. When a horse has his shoes pulled at the end of a season's hard work and is turned out for a well-earned rest, the unshod hoof will tend to expand somewhat as the frog and hoof come into contact with the ground, and when taken up again into work the hoof will not always have exactly the same measurements it had earlier on.

Hot shoeing will ensure that a perfect fit is obtained right at the outset of training.

Even with the ideal hoof, endurance horses have to contend with a variety of types of going, some of them very slippery. To cope with these, several additional aids to shoeing can be employed. Where use of roads is excessive with a horse that is very heavy on shoes, or where the going is very rocky and abrasive, the shoe requires a longer than normal life span. You can add steel tips to the toe, and/or extra steel to each heel; this considerably extends the life of the shoe but provides no extra grip.

Borium. For both grip and good wear I find the ideal answer is Horseshoe Borium. It is expensive, putting up the cost of shoeing considerably, but it does triple the life of shoes so that the same set may be removed and reset several times. Borium also affords tremendous grip because it is annealed to the shoe by a special welding process—the Borium is heated so the carborundum crystals mix with the steel of the shoe. It is these crystals that give extra traction and life as they are exceptionally hard wearing, and as the surface wears away, more crystals are exposed so that good traction is constantly there.

Although Borium generally both adds traction and lengthens the life of the shoe, it can be specifically adapted to either one of those two purposes. For extra life weld 1 inch of Borium to the shoe on either side of the heel and at the toe. For added traction smaller, stud-shaped pieces of Borium are welded to the shoe in four places, one on each side of the heel and two, an inch apart, at the toe. In this case the Borium is raised above the shoe surface, but the spacing prevents the horse from being thrown forward as he can be with normal studs.

Studs. When extra grip is needed, the use of studs can be advantageous, but most have the disadvantages of throwing the horse's weight forward and putting strain on tendons. If they absolutely have to be used because of the type of ground, have them fitted early in training so the horse becomes used to them and there is no sudden strain just prior to the ride. Jumping studs are not suitable for endurance horses. They bite deeply into soft going and if used constantly would produce tendon strains as they elevate the heel considerably. Road studs give adequate grip on road and slippery rocks but bite into soft going, which could be a disadvantage. Plug studs, set into the shoe and wearing with it, with no appreciable raising of heel level, afford road and rock grip. They provide no grip on other going, but if studs have to be used these are the best.

Calkins. These afford extra grip but should always be used in conjunction with rolled toes; otherwise jarring tendons will cause stresses that under hard use could result in lameness. This is because the toe bears the brunt of the weight when the heel is raised.

Earlier I mentioned that the ideal hoof grows between ¼ and ⅝ inch a month. If a horse's hoof growth is poor, the cause could be some lack in his overall diet, as hooves reflect feeding levels in their growth and construction, just as human nails reflect general health. If diet is the problem, it can be rectified by proper attention to the "inner horse." If growth still remains slow and poor, it can be stimulated by applying a mild blister to the coronet. However, care should be exercised that the resulting new growth is not thin and correspondingly weak. In this case applications should be stopped and veterinary advice sought as to the proper treatment. It is absolutely no good applying salves or hoof preparation to the hoof itself; all they will do is to give the hoof a well-cared-for appearance.

There are certain types of hoof which it is best to avoid when choosing a horse. If the hooves have thin walls or the feet are shallow or boxy, it will not be until you have well and truly used your horses that any resulting weaknesses will show up. Some horses with far from ideal hooves are able to perform well, particularly if helped in one of the ways open to the owner. A good farrier can always advise his client of what will minimize such defects and, if they were brought on in the first place by poor shoeing or lack of care, many of them will eventually shrink or disappear.

Shallow hooves. The sole of the shallow, fleshy, or flat hoof is too close to the ground, predisposing the horse to sole bruising. This could rule out competitive endurance events, since some of the terrain to be covered is bound to be stony. To help a horse overcome the disadvantage of shallow hooves, the farrier can shoe him with a shoe made of wide stock, ¾ to 1 inch wide, which will have part of the bearing surface on the wall and part on the sole. There will be less hoof expansion and the sole will be better elevated from the ground, reducing the likelihood of stone bruising.

Shallow feet with dropped or low soles can be protected by the fitting of a metal or plastic plate between shoe and hoof. Leather is also commonly used but, particularly if you live in an area that has considerable rainfall, it has the disadvantage that when it gets wet it swells, pulling on clenches, and, when it subsequently dries out, the shoe is often found to be prematurely loose. All pads should be packed with pine tar and oakum, otherwise foreign matter can enter at the frog. However, before having any pads fitted, check on the ride rules. Although most rides permit the use of pads, others require horses to perform without any aids that could cover up defects. Otherwise the horse that had feet that were not truly up to the work of endurance riding would have an advantage over his unprotected competitors.

Pads can have their disadvantages. I recall a case on the Asheville, North Carolina, ride in which my Standardbred, Magnet Regent, placed in the Lightweight Division. A horse that had done extremely well on the East Coast 100 Miler Circuit was shod with leather pads for the stony mountain tracks. At the first night's check the horse gave the judges a hard time deciding if she was perfectly sound. They had her trotted back and forth many times. From my horse's stable I listened instead of looking, and just discernible was a very, very minute discrepancy in sound as she trotted over the hard surface. When she was pronounced lame and withdrawn from the ride, her shoe was pulled and a minuscule piece of grit was found between pad and hoof. Leather pads cost this horse the probable Ride Championship as she had been convincingly winning these awards at previous rides.

If a horse does have soft soles, they can be toughened by a gradual process of riding him over increasingly stonier ground. I have ridden over many types of going, most recently on Exmoor in Somerset in England. There the going can be pretty punishing to the underparts of a horse's hoof, but if the sole is toughened, it will, barring accidents, stand up to the terrain. Horses used only on soft, spongy going will not develop tough feet, whereas it is widely acknowledged that in the wild, or semiwild, state, horses that have to cover rocky and stony ground develop amazingly tough hooves.

Thin-walled hooves. Shallow feet often go with thin walls, and this thinness means that pressure is concentrated on a limited surface area; it may result in corns. Some thin walls are very strong, but they are often weaker in construction, and too thin a wall leaves less area for the nails to be inserted, with more likelihood of nail binding. This occurs when nails are placed too close to the hoof's inner structure, putting pressure on the sensitive laminae. In addition, a thin wall can lead to overexpansion of the hoof because it is not strong enough to withstand the strain of very hard work. When a horse with thin-walled hooves is shod, correspondingly thin nails should be used to reduce hoof splitting.

Boxy hooves. These are the complete opposite to shallow feet. They are usually deep and very narrow, and are often combined with contracted heels. One of the most common disadvantages of boxy hooves is that excessive strain is put on the tendons. Also, because of the upright pastern and shoulder (the hoof angle is followed through in the line of pastern and shoulder), the action will cause jarring and concussion because there is not enough flexion from the pastern to help absorb the impact. As well as being deleterious to the horse, this makes for a tiring ride.

One frequent cause of boxy hooves is dumping, i.e., setting back of the shoe and rasping the hoof to fit it. Over a period, normal hooves shod in this manner will become more upright and develop a boxy shape. Contracted heels are often the result of fitting too narrow shoes that do not allow for proper hoof expansion. To help counteract both these faults, it is helpful to pare the heels as low to the ground as possible without putting undue strain on the flexor tendons. This enables the frog to play its proper role as a shock absorber and, if used in conjunction with a wide heel on the shoes, will encourage the hoof to expand.

Never knowingly buy a horse with even a slight defect. However, if you already own such an animal, there are several corrective methods available that will either minimize the defect or, if it is not severe, counteract it altogether.

Overreach can be helped by dropping the shoe behind the toe and leaving the toe ¼ inch over the shoe edge. Should the horse still strike himself, damage will not be so severe, and with the weight of the shoe slightly set back the overreach action may be counteracted. Also, the use of "trailers" on the hind shoes can be beneficial. Trailers can often be used to advantage with a horse which is cow-hocked and/or interferes in his action behind, the placing and weight of the trailer helping him to track slightly wider than he would without it.

Brushing can be helped by using a feather-edged shoe and setting the side of the shoe in a fraction so that the extreme inside edge of the hoof carries no metal. It should be remembered that even with a feather-edged shoe constant abrasion from hard going will sharpen the edge, so it will need rasping to keep it smooth. I carry a rasp as part of my grooming equipment on rides so that at halfway halts, if the route has been over roads or stony ground, I can rerasp the edge till rounded and slick. Sometimes even the best tracking horse will knock himself if stones shift suddenly, or if there is very holding going such as sucking clay. Again trailers are sometimes helpful with brushing.

Toe dragging can be helped by normal rolled toe shoes, as can the horse that merely wears his shoes heavily at the toe. Some horses that drag their toes lack sufficient hock flexion, and it is helpful to accentuate the rolling by actually drawing the metal upward to protect the toe.

If the horse is heavy on one side of his shoe, it may be indicative of uneven trimming, which can be rectified, or it may be the result of uneven action. More seriously, it could be a sign of sidebones or ringbone; these will develop into lameness. To help counteract uneven wear, the side that wears most should be made of a wider stock than the other, so handmade shoes and hot shoeing are necessary.

In conclusion, if we consider how small a part of the horse's anatomy the hoof is, this chapter may seem inordinately long and detailed. But of all aspects of a horse's conformation, the hoof is one of the most, if not the most, important in the endurance horse's makeup. To repeat my opening phrase, "No hoof, no horse."

General Conditioning

HAVING selected your endurance mount, you must plan a training program; once you have started you must stick to your plan though this should be flexible enough to permit alterations during the buildup period. The program must be geared to the nature of the work involved. The training of any competitive horse should be designed so as not to bore the animal, who would then become stale, giving less than his best. You should realize at the outset of training that not all horses need the same length of preparation, nor identical workouts. Their physical and mental makeup will dictate to a large extent the type of conditioning necessary.

There are absolutely no shortcuts in endurance fitness preparation. Too hurried a program will result in the horse's being subjected to too great a stress, possibly resulting in a physical breakdown early in a ride or a complete breakdown after the stresses of competition have ceased.

Often a visit to base stables at a competitive long-distance ride reveals a completely different picture from that presented during the ride itself. Some horses, apparently fighting fit en route, show fatigue and stress symptoms later on, while others, who seemed only moderate performers, prove to have suffered no setbacks and are calm, relaxed, and quite obviously ready for more.

A very important aspect of training should be to bring the horse through his work with no undue stress. For this the person who is to ride the horse in competition should also be the one who conditions him. One reason for this is that an unfit rider could hamper a very fit horse, particularly by a poor weight displacement, which can lead to back lesions or bruising. As the rider tires he gradually, without realizing it, ceases to ride in rhythm with the horse and uses the animal purely as a prop for his own fatigue.

Another reason is that during training the rider will learn to recognize all sorts of subtle indications as to how the horse is feeling and using himself, and will notice stress symptoms immediately and ease up temporarily, thus conserving energy instead of pushing the horse and risking damage to him. Unless the rider does the training, he will not know how to pace the horse over a course, and may burn him out in the first few miles. Alternatively he may drop too far behind schedule, and have to push on relentlessly in the last stages, bringing the horse in with bad heart and respiration rates that will not show adequate recovery, and thus will jeopardize the animal's chances of passing the veterinary examination.

Before embarking on any training program, make sure the horse is in good physical condition, recently wormed and, if an older horse, has had his teeth checked by the vet. If he has been purchased with endurance riding in mind, have him thoroughly checked for suitability before paying for him. Also, bearing in mind the horse will be covering considerably more miles than he would during normal work, make prior bookings with your farrier. It is no good embarking on a work schedule only to find it interrupted for days at a time because you cannot get an appointment for shoeing.

At the outset the horse should be carrying enough spare flesh so he does not run up light during early training. At the finish of training the horse should be very hard, with no excess soft fat to impede him, but he should not look whittled down as he will need a little reserve to call upon.

The type of horse I prefer working with as an endurance prospect is one that does not run to fat and, even when idle, maintains considerable working condition and muscular tone. This type usually possesses a keen but stable disposition. In Britain the top ride so far has been the two-day Golden Horseshoe Event run over 75 very testing miles—50 miles the first day and 25 miles the second day. I like four months to prepare for the speeds of 6 to 7½ mph necessary for a Bronze or Silver award. A longer preparation period should be allowed for the required Gold time of 9 mph. However, there is provision for occasional "rest breaks" in this training schedule, as continuous work might bring the horse to his peak too early, causing him to begin to tire of it at the time when he most needed his zest for competition. For the 40-mile qualifying rides at 7 mph which each Golden Horseshoe entrant has to complete, a training period of roughly eight weeks is about right. For Endurance Horse and Pony Society rides and similar events, where an outright winner is declared, the vets have to look for minute stress symptoms to separate the exceptionally fit from the very fit, so a slightly longer period of slow conditioning work at the outset is beneficial. With the American 100-mile three-day competitive trail rides and the 50- to 100-mile one-day endurance events, training is geared somewhat differently from that for the British Golden Horseshoe ride, which falls between them. In a subsequent chapter more specific notes relating to different rides are tabulated with attention paid to the initial pleasure rides which are a means of working up to competitive events.

If your horse is not of the preferred type, or if he is straight off grass in summer, is put into work after a complete layoff in winter, is grossly overweight, or is a younger animal, it is best to take longer; but with the mature horse of the type already mentioned that is used to light, regular work, shorter periods are suitable. One word of caution regarding breed characteristics. The Arabian is acknowledged by the relevant equine authorities to be a late-maturing breed, so where a five-year-old of a different breed may be approaching maturity the Arabian still has a lot of making up to do. In the three years I have ridden Nizzolan in the Golden Horseshoe I have noticed a marked escalation in stamina and drive to compete, and also in the amount of vitality still present at the end of the 75 miles. When he was a five-year-old, I planned simply to complete the course, which was in Sussex over very rolling hill country. He gained a Silver, with an average speed of 8.3 mph and full vet marks. The next year, though the ride venue moved to Gloucestershire and the far more taxing Cotswold Hills, he completed the 75 miles with an overall speed of 9.26 mph, a Gold and full marks. The next Golden Horseshoe was held in Somerset over the extremely rugged terrain of the Exmoor National Park. Here owing to the severity of the going the speed was lowered to 8 mph for a Gold. On the first day we averaged 8.3 mph and on the second day 8.5 mph, achieving a Gold and full vet marks. On this ride, even though the going was very tough, Nizzolan finished at a very strong canter with 15 minutes in hand. The aftereffects of the ride were absolutely nonexistent; he was out in his home paddock loose and moving very freely the day after. I have gone into this in some detail to explain the differences that can be expected as a horse matures. In retrospect, I feel that as a five-year-old he could not have done Gold speed with full veterinary marks over the Exmoor course. Yet as a seven-year-old he finished the course with many miles left in him, and at award-giving time, when there had been a long trailer trip back to base stables and a three-hour time lapse in which any aftereffects might be expected to show, he was still fresh and quite willing to move out freely; in fact he showed polite but very definite interest in the mare with whom he had traveled the whole of the last 25 miles over Exmoor—hardly the sign of a tired horse. Some American breeds, notably the Quarterhorse and Appaloosa, seem to mature much earlier than the Arabian, at least outwardly, but this does not mean that the maximum should be asked of a five-year-old in his first permitted year of competition. No horse truly matures that early, and if not pushed too hard early in his career, he will last longer and still be competing into his teens.

The endurance horse should use himself to the best possible advantage in all his work. If he is lacking in suppleness or not schooled enough in taking the correct lead at the beginning, a thorough basic schooling period prior to entering into endurance training will more than pay off.

This book is not intended as an equitation manual; but sound schooling is the first step to good performance and the same tenet that applies to the horse goes for the rider. Bad riding can prevent a good horse from giving his best performance, and a mediocre horse from even getting to the starting post.

Particular attention should be paid to certain points. Make sure that the horse moves forward freely, using his hindquarters to propel himself. All motive power should come from behind and the weight be borne mainly by the forehand. If the forehand does double duty, the horse will not only be uncomfortable to ride, possibly hanging on your hands, but also be more prone to front-leg ailments as they take the brunt of the work.

He should be schooled to give a lightgoing, mannerly ride both in company and by himself. For this, he needs to be relaxed but alert enough to act on his rider's instructions instantaneously. A tense horse wastes precious energy, and a lazy animal wears out his rider. Of the two I would rather have the tense horse, as proper schooling can nearly always change this for the better. A really lazy horse is useless as he will never enter into the spirit of endurance riding, and the whole thing becomes too much of an effort for the rider, who cannot help being discouraged by a consistently ungenerous performance from his mount. On the other hand, some apparently lazy horses are merely unschooled animals who have never had to exert themselves, or have become so bored with dull routine they cease thinking for themselves. These can be cured and enlivened by an interesting program coupled with firm, purposeful riding.

I find that animals suffering from flightiness, tenseness, lack of concentration, playful shying, or just plain lack of interest are entirely changed by a season of competitive endurance work. During this time they come to realize they have a job to do and need to concentrate all their energies to produce maximum effort with minimum fatigue.

In actual competition the trot will be the main gait used, as it both covers the ground and spreads the horse's work load evenly, thus minimizing fatigue. Normally only English or flat-saddle riders rise to the trot, and though many western horsemen have found that rising to the trot over extended periods alleviates strain for both themselves and their horses, newcomers to the sport might not realize that this is preferable. If a rider attempts to sit tight when the horse is using a ground-eating trot, he will become uncomfortable and also bump repeatedly on the horse's back, with the result that at the end of the day the horse could have a very sore back indeed. The alternative is to stand slightly in the stirrups and take the strain on your own leg muscles, but over a period of time this can wear out the rider; furthermore if the horse should stumble, the rider is not in such a good position to help him recover his balance. Rising to the trot becomes so much a part of the rhythm of riding that it is automatic, so western riders new to endurance riding would be well advised to accustom themselves to rising.

When trotting make sure you change the diagonal frequently to give each pair of legs equal work. Some, but not all, horses react to continuous use of one diagonal to carry the work load by stiffening on the load-carrying legs. This does not normally show until the animal has had time to rest up, and in a two-day ride this could be detrimental to a perfect veterinary score. The same goes for cantering (loping in western parlance), as continuous use of one lead puts undue stress on that particular set of muscles and the weight-bearing leg gets overworked.

The endurance season usually starts around March, when the first rides are scheduled, so conditioning means winter training. In England, where hunting is still a widespread sport, hunting fitness is an asset; but, good as it is, it is insufficient for endurance riding because, even though total hunting mileage is considerable, a hunter is rarely asked to maintain a steady pace hour after hour. In America in hunting areas such as Maryland, Virginia, Pennsylvania, the Piedmont of North Carolina, and also parts of California, training can be varied and therefore more fun, with hunting providing part of the exercise, but it should be used in conjunction with the other parts of the training schedule. In some areas training schedules will have to be worked out according to local climatic conditions. Bear in mind that much training will be done at steady speeds of between 6 and 8 mph. On paper this doesn't look very impressive, but in practice, over a course of 40 miles or more, it is very telling on a horse. So during training, nothing beats a program incorporating long, steady well-paced rides.

I do not like systems of training specifying a certain number of weeks with a given number of hours and miles broken down into given minutes of walk, trot, canter. I consider this too rigid by far and in some cases it can defeat the objective of getting a horse to the ride at his peak, really fresh both mentally and physically. Have a skeleton routine incorporating steady buildup to peak performance, but be prepared to change it according to the way your mount reacts.

The type of work done is largely dictated by the terrain, and the more varied the training ground the fresher your mount will be mentally, and the tougher in legs and wind.

Here a divergence into some of my own experiences on the American 100-mile competitive trail rides may prove helpful. Many riders worry that their home territory does not offer enough variation, particularly in regard to hill work or work in very holding conditions. Although it is an advantage to have the ideal training ground, it does not necessarily follow that only horses trained on them will be successful.

I lived in North Carolina near Jacksonville, where it is extremely flat. The going I rode over was mostly packed sand roads or woodland grass and sand, interspersed with sandy tracks with light, nonholding footing. The first 100-miler I tackled was in Florida where the going is again sand for the most part, but of the deep, holding variety, giving in some places exceptionally deep and heavy going with a correspondingly severe pull on muscles and tendons, and forcing the horses to use their lungs to capacity. In consecutive years I rode a Standardbred six-year-old mare and a five-year-old Arabian stallion. Both horses coped very well with the conditions. In complete contrast to Florida I rode the Standardbred in the Asheville 100 Miler in North Carolina's Smoky Mountains. She was a horse bred in the lowlands, but she coped beautifully with the change of terrain.

Where the countryside stays virtually the same for hundreds of miles, going to different terrain for practice is out of the question. However, if you live in the lowlands, extra care must be taken in preparing the horse for hills or holding going. The horse that is prepared well can succeed but the horse that has had some of his training skimped will certainly be under stress in more severe conditions, even though he may perform adequately on home territory.

In England most Golden Horseshoe and other endurance rides incorporate a considerable percentage of very hilly country except where this is impossible, as in the flat Fen district of

Cambridgeshire or the New Forest in Hampshire. I do not find my horses unduly stressed when tackling the hilly rides. Although they do not have hills of any degree to work over at home in the New Forest, they do receive careful conditioning prior to the rides, which enables them to cope with new situations very well. A friend of mine from Scotland was worried about this, as she lives on the coastal plain in Aberdeenshire where most of the going is relatively flat, but she found on coming to the hilly Exmoor Golden Horseshoe that her horse coped admirably.

Early training calls for plenty of walking and steady trotting, which will muscle up your horse and also stabilize him. You don't want him to get the idea that long rides mean one prolonged, undisciplined scamper to eat up the miles. If you allow him to do this, there is the risk that he may run up light, and also that he may overtax a frame as yet not properly conditioned to the strain of sustained speed.

During the first weeks step up both time and mileage gradually. There is no need to stick to the old-fashioned way of weeks of endless walking before proceeding to trot and canter; a horse that soft, even with the excuses of being just off grass or out of condition from a complete rest period, wouldn't be a very good prospect. Also lack of variety will bore him, making him either lethargic or, on the contrary, constantly looking for games to play which could turn into vices.

The horse that has been completely idle should have a couple of weeks of daily riding starting with an hour a day before he is put into more exacting training for his long-distance work. By the end of two weeks he should be able to take a three-hour steady jaunt covering about 15 miles. Or you may wish to bring him up more slowly, taking longer, if you can ride only every other day. In winter training for those riders who have a regular job the amount of daylight plays a large part in governing how much time there is available for riding other than on weekends. As the evenings lengthen the training program can include daily rides, with weekends being used for the more lengthy workouts. But do remember throughout that the horse, particularly the endurance horse, isn't a delicate animal. He is a work animal, though this fact is often forgotten now that he is used almost exclusively for pleasure.

Care should be taken, particularly at first, to toughen the skin under saddle and girth, as soft skin on an unfit horse can chafe very easily. Two aids in this process are surgical spirit and methylated spirit. Of the two, I prefer the first, as some horses are leery of odd smells and surgical spirit is odorless. While on the subject of tender skins, a word about girths and girth covers. I find string, nylon, or mohair girths softer than leather, less likely to chafe, and easier to keep clean. A leather girth costs several times the price of the other varieties; the money is better spent on several so that one can always be clean and ready. Girth covers are useful with a horse whose hair, however careful you are, tends to rub slightly. Nizzolan's does this during the latter stages of ride training as the hours he is under saddle build up, since no matter how I fix the girth or how soft it is it will still move very slightly with the horse's motion and rhythmic breathing. To prevent this I have made some very soft acrylic fiber girth covers that slip over the girth and cover the thin hair patches. After a few days with these covers the hair grows out to normal length once more. I also vary the English girth billets that are used. Sometimes I use the first and second and sometimes the second and third to minimize wear on one particular area. With a western saddle the most likely place for a hair rub—no matter how well the tack fits—is where the cinch ring comes into contact with the horse's skin. Soft-covered, leather-backed protectors can be used to minimize this. However, these minor hair clippings only seem to occur in the extremely fine-coated horses such as Arabians, whose winter coats are like most other horses' summer coats and whose summer coats are exceptionally thin.

Vary the horse's routine with occasional spells of schoolwork. When time does not permit you to ride, a longeing session is beneficial provided the horse works on the longe, bending correctly and using himself from behind, not merely circling in a dilatory fashion with his hocks trailing.

Although there will be some days when the rider's schedule must be interrupted, it is all too easy for one day to become two, and for training to become a hit-or-miss affair. A tight check should be kept on such tendencies, or fitness will not proceed beyond moderate, and if such lapses occur later on in training, it could result in regression for the horse.

It isn't only the length of workouts that counts but the way the horse uses himself. One working properly by engaging his hindquarters puts all his energies into forward movement. The horse who is always on his forehand hammers into the ground and tires his rider and himself without achieving true fitness. Instead he puts excessive strain on shoulders and forelimbs while the hindquarters remain slack, lacking the good muscular development necessary for endurance work. Watch your mount's manner of tackling the job, and carry out the general schooling while trail riding. It is absolutely no good schooling the horse in a ring on home ground and allowing him to become dilatory and undisciplined when he is put on the trail. This is one of the main reasons why some horses are ill-mannered in company or away from the barn.

The rider who trains alone most of the time should try teaming up with others occasionally, as the horse that has gone stale solo frequently finds new energy in company, which brings out his competitive spirit and keeps his interest keen. Conversely, if you normally ride in company, give your mount some solo work because there will inevitably be times on competitive rides when it is better for him to travel alone. The horse must be relaxed during solo work; otherwise you may have troubles with your mount fretting to catch up or going behind the bit and waiting for a friend to join him.

It is rare to find two horses with exactly matching strides and two riders who plan their routes identically. I do a fair percentage of home training across New Forest territory with a friend, and although we do ride together for the greater part of the distance, my stallion, Nizzolan, has a slower, more rolling canter than hers has, which takes very little out of him, and he is faster than hers when extending at the trot. When we wish to pace our horses individually we split temporarily, then team up again when opportunity occurs. The horses appreciate each other's company, but adapt easily to working alone. Normally Nizzolan takes the lead, but occasionally he falls back and relaxes, leaving the added mental strain of being the leader to the first in line.

I have a young paint pony, Katchina, who had his first season in 1973 when as a five-year-old he started a British Qualifier very much the newcomer. He used the more experienced horses on the ride to show him the ropes and tow him along, then got completely lit up when changing places and forged ahead at a very strong pace for the last 12 miles without adverse effect.

Endurance horses must be able to go it alone, but there are times when a tiring horse finds fresh stimulus if he can team up with a stronger-striding animal, and many high placing awards in endurance riding are due to just this factor in the final stages. Show consideration to the other rider; he may not welcome having another horse along, particularly if his own mount travels best alone.

On one competitive ride, I rode with a friend; both our mares were approximately the same height and similar in stride and speed, with comparably keen dispositions. Toward the end of the ride we overtook a considerably slower, stocky gelding. When we slowed down, along came the gelding to join us, which was well enough, but after that each time we put on a spurt so did he, slowing down only when we did but managing to do so in front of our mares. Each time he did so he got progressively slower, and when we made a move to pull out and overtake he speeded up just enough to keep us behind, then slowed down once more. This was having anything but a good effect on two free-striding, keen mares, so we pulled out and set such a hot pace that the gelding was forced to fall back.

I mention this to underline the point that it is not always wise or considerate to try to team up with horses who are not comparable in stride and speed. It could make a keen horse waste precious energy being held back for a slower companion. Should a moderate-paced animal try stepping out above the speed at which he is comfortable and relaxed, he risks burning himself out too soon, whereas individual pacing of the ride gets the job done while conserving precious energy. On the Exmoor Golden Horseshoe in 1974 Nizzolan teamed up with a very fit, game part-Arabian mare, Candy's Evening Star, toward the latter part of the first day's 50 miles, and as we were both aiming for Gold we rode together the whole of the next morning's 25 miles. The horses worked antagonistically to some degree but this was to our advantage, as neither horse wanted to be runner-up, and when one of our respective mounts would pause for a bit, the temporarily stronger horse gave the other an incentive to keep up the average. However, the mare had frequent spells of walking when we split up, and Nizzolan used his special endurance trot, which comes more easily than a walk when he is momentarily tired. He goes into this of his own accord and I have learned to leave well enough alone, for when he gets his second wind he automatically picks up the faster gait and speed we were doing before.

While on the subject of pacing a ride, note that it is important to have an approximate idea of how many miles per hour your horse is traveling, and this can be achieved only by a thorough knowledge of your own mount and consistent riding. A good way of learning your horse's individual speeds at trot and canter is to have a car pace you at different gaits on ground suitable for both car and horse. Once you know these speeds in relation to the horse's gaits, you will realize the value of prior schooling, for it is effective schooling allied with long, steady periods of work that stabilizes the gaits. When asked for a slow 6- or 7-mph trot the horse should maintain it until geared up to a stronger striding 9 or 10 mph. Cantering speeds should be aimed at between 10 and 12 mph. This is a good rolling-on gait without excessive waste of energy since it keeps the horse calm while still covering the miles.

In endurance riding, as opposed to general schooling and hacking, one gait should be maintained for appreciable distances. In this way the fitness, muscling, and conditioning begin to pay off, and at the same time you are building up the horse's wind by getting him to breathe deeply, using his lungs to capacity. Consistent riding will keep the horse calm but alert, and a horse allowed to settle into a strong rhythmic stride will use considerably less energy than one whose rider constantly changes the horse's gait so that he becomes tense, never achieving the almost machinelike rhythm of the experienced animal.

To help toughen the horse's legs and feet, vary the ground

over which you work him as much as possible. On rides in unknown territory you could meet hard, flinty going, or the other extreme of heavy holding ground, with all the variations in between. If the horse is used to varied terrain, his tendons and ligaments will stay clean, his hooves will be tougher, and the concussion on hard ground will be less of a problem.

Another advantage of using as much variety as possible in training is that it teaches a horse to look where he is going. Some horses have a natural gift for being clever on their feet, but others seem to think the rider is there to support them over every hillock and depression. I have one of each: Katchina, who is naturally nifty and perfectly safe over the roughest ground without any help from his rider, and Nizzolan, who at the very beginning of his endurance life needed careful watching. Happily a season's hard hunting, together with the occasional colt hunt, in which the year's crop of pony foals and their dams are rounded up on the New Forest, changed this. On these colt hunts semiwild ponies go hell-for-leather across open forest and it takes a quick horse to stay with them, sometimes having to put the brakes on and cut back to put a breakaway into the herd. On endurance rides Nizzolan now senses the need for keeping his wits about him and is absolutely surefooted, but on ordinary rides if he becomes bored, he will invariably trip into an invisible crater. Magnet Regent has an almost machinelike manner of going, but is concerned with one thing only—getting from point A to point B as quickly as possible. She uses herself economically, but does need watching if the going is rough. I think this stems from her breed, which naturally moves close to the ground, and, over the centuries, has been developed for speed, not for a handy way of going. Her toughness more than makes up for the rider's having to be on the watch for hazards underfoot.

I have talked to other riders who have very alert, competitive horses, and they remark that on nontraining or noncompetitive rides, when the horses know they are just out for a trail ride, they are also a bit slapdash about how they cover the ground. A seasoned endurance horse senses the urgency of the competition and, once the first few miles are behind, really comes alive, enthusiastically forging ahead.

Once the horse is fit, demand the best from him in the form of very active rides of 25 miles and over if you are aiming for 100 miles in three days, longer if pulling for endurance rides of 50 to 100 miles in one day. The greater part of the mileage should be done at a ground-eating trot, interspersed with strong, lengthy canters. When walking give him a loose rein, as this will enable him to stretch his neck muscles and relax physically and mentally.

The variation from one horse to another is immense, but broadly speaking the horse's working week should be six days on, one day off. If you plan to enter the really tough rides or keep a horse competitively fit for the whole season, you will benefit from a different work schedule, and I will deal with this later.

Whatever length of ride you intend tackling, make sure in advance that your horse is really up to it. I like to test my horse by a training ride covering two-thirds to three-quarters of the forthcoming event's total distance shortly before the ride itself. How close to the event one does this and the distance one should tackle depend on which event one is aiming for. These points are also developed later.

It is important to bear in mind that you must not bring your mount to the start of any competitive ride stale and past his peak. This is a mistake a lot of novice riders make. They train hard right up to the event itself, only to have the horse start jaded and sometimes a little leg weary into the bargain. Always ease up in the last few days prior to any event. The horse's whole mental outlook will be brighter, and his physical condition will be that much sharper if he is not subjected to undue stress.

Training for Competitive Trail Rides

THIS chapter deals with how to vary your training program for specific events. Obviously the length of the ride you are aiming at will affect the amount and type of training. It is a waste of time, energy, and feed (most important, considering present-day exorbitant costs) to do more than is necessary, and excessive conditioning wears a horse physically and mentally, souring his enthusiasm. Underconditioning, on the other hand, is nothing short of maltreatment and is the prime reason for attrition in the longer endurance and competitive trail rides.

Pleasure Rides Varying From 20 to 30 Miles

Most of these do not have a specified speed. They are normally run at a rate of between 5 and 6 mph. For the shorter distance a horse needs only moderate conditioning. If he is already used to light hacking covering about 6 to 10 miles four times a week, an extra two weeks' work, during which time the distances are lengthened, will sharpen him up to coping with the 20 miles. Up to that distance, stress symptoms are unlikely to show if the horse is moderately fit. Riding several times a week and stepping up time and distance during the last period have the effect of toning muscles, strengthening legs, and toughening skin areas over his back and around his girth.

When you progress from 20- to 30-mile events the training should be taken more seriously. This means increasing the distance traveled on the longer training rides and incorporating into such rides several uninterrupted miles of steady trotting at around 8 mph, interspersed with the occasional sharp canter of about a mile and plenty of free-striding walking. In this way the average of 5 to 6 mph can be maintained without difficulty, and the extra stresses involved in doing a straight 30 miles are taken care of by the gradual buildup in general condition.

It should take about a month to bring a horse from ordinary light hacking fitness to a condition in which he can easily tackle 30 miles at 6 mph. This type of event is very suitable for riders with limited time, as the work schedule needed is not so severe or time-consuming as that for longer, tougher rides. If the horse does well in a 20- to 30-mile pleasure ride, it will give the rider an incentive to enter the longer rides and find the extra time necessary for more intensive conditioning.

Once you decide to train for 30 miles, the work schedule should include at least two longish rides a week, plus three days of ordinary exercise. Do not make the mistake of thinking that because your horse is now approaching the fringe of long-distance riding his routine must include long rides every day. Up to this point his work schedule will dovetail quite easily with that of the weekend rider, as weekday rides can be kept down to the hour and a half limit and the weekends used for lengthier rides. At this stage two days a week should still be left free. Vary his work, using the shorter rides for sharp work. On the days when you have time for the longer, more leisurely rides, the thing to aim for is not speed but consistency, at the same time getting the horse used to bearing weight for several hours. In referring to riding at speed versus leisurely riding, I do not mean either exhaustive speed at one end of the scale or an aimless potter at the other. On the longer, more leisurely rides the horse should still be induced to step forward forcefully, using himself to the best advantage and employing a long stride. If you aim for an average of 5 to 6 mph this can be done comfortably while maintaining a decent amount of impulsion by using lengthy periods of steady trotting and a ground-covering walk. On the other hand endurance horses, except for the occasional pipe opener of a gallop, should not be worked for any length of time at average speeds in excess of 10 or, at the most, 12 mph. Even with a very fit horse too much continued speedwork will induce mental and physical stresses, particularly in the legs, that could have been avoided with a more conservative training program. Also general bodily condition will suffer as, even with superb feeding, a horse will not maintain that little bit of extra condition needed as a reserve to be called on when energy expenditure is greater than nutritional intake. In Britain veterinarians have found that when contending for the Golden Horseshoe at 9 mph over a stiff course of 75 miles, horses that averaged 9 to 10 mph have racked up far better veterinary scores than those who burnt themselves out over the first 25 miles; they would have to drop to 7 mph or less for the rest of the first day and would be unable to produce more than a ticking-over speed on the second day's 25-mile leg, altogether bringing them in at an average of 6 to 7 mph for the lower award of a Bronze.

A rough work guide for the 30-miler could be:

Monday (after the long rides of the weekend). An easy hour of walking and trotting, aiming to cover about 6 miles, prior to his day off.
Tuesday. Rest day.
Wednesday. Approximately an hour and a half of steady riding, aiming to cover about 10 miles.
Thursday. About two hours' steady work, including a couple of miles of sharp travel to keep the horse mentally fresh.
Friday. Rest day.
Saturday. A ride of 15-plus miles, taking around three hours.
Sunday. A distance of between 20 and 25 miles taken steadily.

During the weekend just prior to the 30-mile event, do at least one steady 25-mile ride, and slightly step up his midweek workouts in distance but not speed, with the exception of the day before the ride when the horse should be ridden lightly just to keep him limbered up. On ride day go steadily, particularly if it is the horse's introduction to long-distance riding in company, as this sets the pattern for his mental and physical energy expenditure and gives a good indication as to how he will use himself in future, more taxing events.

If you intend to go on to the more difficult events, the more of these shorter rides you can participate in and the more varied the terrain and different the equine company the better, as your horse will soon learn to settle and use himself sparingly, not being upset by the unusual surroundings and activities. At these events it is easy to spot the experienced horse, both by his attitude to the whole thing and by the way he rates on the course himself as regards speed and gait, without seeming to get any visible instructions from the rider. To ride such a horse is an experience in itself, as you feel that true partnership which is one of the main attractions of the sport.

Competitive Trail Rides

After taking part in the one-day pleasure rides of between 20 and 30 miles you may want to think about entering a competitive ride. There is a tremendous variety to choose from, but broadly speaking they fall into two main categories: endurance rides, covering 50 to 100 miles in one day and judged on a time basis, the fastest fit horse being the winner; and competitive trail rides, ranging from 25 miles in one day to 100 miles in three days, and judged on a time-plus-condition basis, with penalties given for too high or too low a speed. Further on in the book there is a chapter giving a more detailed description of the main events open to long-distance trail riders.

For the horse that has been conditioned for the less-taxing shorter pleasure rides, the next logical step up seems to me to be starting conditioning for the one- and two-day competitive trail rides, which fall mainly into the 40/20-mile bracket. It is a big step from pleasure riding to competitive trail riding fitness, but the type of conditioning for the longer pleasure rides prepares the horse for this next stage, requiring only about four weeks to bring him to condition for a one-day 40-miler.

One of the biggest differences between the pleasure and the competitive ride is that the rider now has to be constantly aware of very minor things that before he probably dismissed or maybe didn't even notice. It is on these small points that the veterinary judges will be commenting in their scorecards, and often it is a very slight thing that determines winner, minor placings, and completing horses. Later in the book there is a brief section in note form on some of the things of which any rider should be aware, particularly an endurance and/or competitive trail entrant.

Preparing for the 40-mile competitive trail ride event

means that the horse's work schedule will alter quite considerably from that considered sufficient for the 30-mile pleasure ride. He will now need to work six days on and one day off, the distances will increase, and speeds used will need to rise considerably for part of his mileage.

On paper 6 mph doesn't look much, but in practice you will have found it is quite a considerable speed. Speed rules for competitive trail riding vary, but are likely to be 6½ to 7 mph. That extra speed means that only a really fit horse will come through without showing signs of stress. I reiterate, do not overdo speed by asking the horse for a high output during all his workouts, as he will become a tense, drawn animal instead of one that relaxes and forges comfortably ahead.

During this training period the 20 miles that initially was the top effort becomes part of the ordinary routine. Several rides of this distance will be needed in the last month, with at least one or two of 30-plus miles. Prior conditioning has accustomed the horse to long rides. Now he has to do distance plus a consistently higher speed. The rider must pay particular attention to rating his horse, and it is worth experimenting with speeds and distances until you easily recognize at approximately what speed your horse is traveling. This will be a much better guide than constant map reference.

In preparing my own horses I work considerable mileage at a strong trot, averaging about 10 mph, which gives quite a bit of leeway for relaxing periods of walking during which the horse recoups energy ready for his next geared-up trotting session. Where terrain permits, I switch to cantering, alternating leads to share work load. When my horse can comfortably cover 32 miles in a four-hour workout and still have plenty of reserve left I know he is ready to do the 40 miles at 7 mph.

Before passing on to the next point, a few words about gaits. No two horses perform identically and the main gait used will be dictated to some degree by the horse's conformation and facility in covering ground, and also of course by the difficulty of the terrain. Bear in mind that the trot is the most economical gait, as it shares the work load equally over the whole of the horse's structure and thereby tires him less than cantering. For true endurance riding nothing beats the trot, but each horse should be treated and worked as an individual. With Nizzolan I find that the canter takes very little out of him on easy going and although I use the trot for the greater percentage of the time, cantering gives both him and me a welcome change. With Magnet Regent I very rarely use the canter, as that Standardbred trot is so smooth and groundcovering; sometimes the canter gives her racetrack ideas. She is easier to rate efficiently at a trot and does not become overexcited as she would in a canter. Other horses, particularly the heavily muscled varieties, may have a rather jarring trot, which is tiring to their riders and wearing on the horse himself, particularly in the front legs. These are better switched to the canter where permissible. However, these types do appreciably better in competitive trail rides in America and in the lower speed brackets of British endurance rides than in true endurance riding, where speed over a long time is necessary. Here the more streamlined horse with less bulk to transport performs better. Do remember that in many cases where a horse seems to have a poor trot it is the result of lack of training, and teaching the horse to use himself will bring out his best work capacity. Many horses that have a poor walk are made to jog instead. It would be much better to teach the horse to extend himself at the walk, thus limbering and conditioning his muscles, rather than permit the cramping type of jog that is hard on both horse and rider. Ideally all gaits in endurance and competitive trail horses should be long, loose, and free-striding, to stretch muscles and keep the stride elastic. This minimizes fatigue, because a free-striding horse never jars himself.

Experience will tell you how much reserve a horse has on hand, but how he looks and behaves provides a good guide. Does he respond to the leg as quickly as before? If in company, is he still competitive? His eye gives an excellent indication of his reserve. If it is still wide open and alert-looking, he is feeling great. If, when he is asked to move on, it looks relatively dull, then fatigue is setting in. Head carriage is another good guide. When a normally gay head carriage lowers, it could be a sign of tiredness, and a horse with a normally low head carriage may indicate fatigue by leaning on the rider's hands.

Each rider should know his own horse's normal attitude

and be able to detect when something is not quite right. The best guides of all to the horse's fitness are his heartbeat and his respiration. The latter is visible and can easily be checked en route. A high heart rate can also be roughly checked by listening close to his girth, just behind the elbow. After going 20 miles at 7 to 8 mph the horse's heart and respiration rates will be up considerably. If after he has rested for ten minutes these rates show no appreciable decrease, then he is not truly fit. If both rates drop rapidly and steadily, the horse is fit and ready for more.

Here, in broad terms, is an outline for average heart and breathing rates for a fit horse. *Heartbeat:* At rest 40 beats to the minute; after fairly hard work about 80 beats to the minute; after extreme energy expenditure this could go over the 100 mark. If a horse's heart refuses to drop rapidly from a very high rate when work ceases, it is a sign of danger. On many rides should the rate not drop to 70 or below after the compulsory rest stops, horses are not permitted to continue. *Respiration rate:* At rest around 16 to the minute, increasing to around 26 to the minute after moderate work and considerably higher after extreme exertion. The horse is in danger when his normal breathing mechanism is insufficient to cope; the signs of this insufficiency will be accompanied by other obvious evidence of a distressed condition.

Normal or near normal rates of both heart and respiration should be reached approximately 30 minutes after exertion ceases when work has been hard but not severe, and within one hour when energy expenditure has been extreme. On rides that have several veterinary checks and rest periods the further on in the ride that these occur the longer recovery will take, as tiredness and stress become more prominent as the mileage adds up.

As a horse progresses in his training and becomes fitter, his original normal heart and breathing rates may show a marked decrease, so the above figures should be taken only as indicative of general rates. They are intended as a rough guide for those unfamiliar with this way of calculating the horse's fitness.

A stethoscope is a very worthwhile investment for any

rider seriously contemplating endurance riding. He can then learn his horse's normal heart rate. This should be taken when the horse is at ease and relaxed in his stable. Sometimes the horse is alarmed the first few times this is done so the rate will rise, but if you do it regularly he will ignore the stethoscope and the rate will remain constant. It pays to get the horse accustomed to this well in advance of any competitive ride, so that the heart rate taken on the ride will be a true indication of his fitness, and no allowances will need to be made for "nerves."

While you are training for a ride it is a good idea to make a practice of taking the horse's heart rate as soon as you finish a strenuous workout and again thirty minutes later. If it has not dropped back to normal or near normal, considerable conditioning is still needed. This is best done when the horse is quiet in his box. Place the stethoscope in the region of the girth just behind and about a hand's breadth above the left elbow. At first it may be difficult to find the right spot. This is easier on some horses than others. I remember one which registered only from a place beneath the girth and I have had to maneuver about with several. Once you have located the beat take the rate for 15 seconds and multiply by four. If the horse will remain absolutely still long enough, you can count for a full minute, but even a muscle twitch can make hearing difficult. At peak fitness Nizzolan shows 32, Katchina 40, and Magnet Regent 36 beats to the minute. Some horses show a considerably higher reading and one I know had a normal reading as low as 28, so the only true guide is your own horse, not a table of statistics.

Many horses' heart rates approximately double after hard work. If the rate goes higher than this, the horse is overtaxed and showing definite signs of stress. After a period of extreme exertion the rider should not be alarmed by a much higher count. However, should the count not start dropping within minutes after ceasing work, the horse is not fit.

If the horse's heart rate shows excellent recovery one day and not the next, look for some other factor that may not be immediately apparent. On one highly competitive ride in 1973 this point was emphasized when several horses known to be fit showed poor recovery. All of these horses, when trotted out after the cooling-out period, proved to be very slightly, almost undetectably, lame. If this happens in training, take warning and start looking for the seat of trouble. It may save you a real problem later on.

An approximate guide to the last month's training for a 40-mile competitive trail ride at 6½ to 7 mph would go something like this:

WEEK 1.

1st day. A steady ride of about 10 miles taking about 90 minutes.

2nd day. Ditto.

3rd day. Sharp ride for about an hour stepping up the pace, covering the same distance as days 1 and 2.

4th day. 15 miles taking about two-and-a-half hours.

5th day. 20–25 miles at approximately 6 mph.

6th day. An hour-and-a-half easy ride in letting down for rest day.

7th day. Rest day.

WEEK 2.

Very similar to week 1 but increasing the distances by 2 to 3 miles on each of the days, keeping one very sharp ride in the schedule and doing 25 miles at 7 mph for day 5.

WEEK 3.

It is time to put the pressure on for three workdays, hack lightly for two, and give the horse two consecutive days to himself with no more than either a light longe or walking exercise to limber him up. He is already fit, and you should not overdo his workouts. Try to make two of the three days of hard work consecutive, covering about 25 miles one day and 20 the next at a little above the 7 mph average. Follow this by a letdown day and then his two days off.

WEEK 4.

If he comes through week 3 bright and eager, you need only keep him ticking over for week 4. During the week prior to the event, taking this to be run on a Saturday, I like to work him moderately on Monday with about 12 miles of steady going, a 20-mile sprint in two-and-a-half hours on Tuesday, an easy ride of one-and-a-half hours on Wednesday, followed by Thursday off, and on Friday a sharp pipe opener of a workout with ample cooling-out time. Then he comes to the ride on Saturday bright and eager.

This is the schedule for a 40-mile-in-one-day ride. Should you decide on a two-day 40/20-miler (or thereabouts) the conditioning will be very little different since this program emphasizes methodical conditioning and is carefully arranged not to overtax the horse. This being so, the 20 miles of day 2 will be taken in stride if he is truly fit, and in effect will tell the veterinary judges which rider has thoroughly and sensibly conditioned his horse, as a fit horse is always ready for more than is asked, and competent training conditions a horse so that he is capable of more than the stipulated minimum requirements.

The foregoing outline is not intended as a rigid guide but it gives a fair idea of how to condition the average, keen but not silly horse. A lethargic animal might well benefit from additional sharp rides to wake him up and a flighty horse might go better if these are used only very sparingly. No program should be so fixed it cannot be altered to meet special circumstances, and the more a rider involves himself with this type of riding the more such conditioning will become second nature to him. Indeed I found it very difficult to actually put down a training schedule as so much of my own work is governed by the instinct that comes from experience and from training my own horses, who virtually tell me if things are proceeding just right by the way they work.

At least once during the later stages of training for a two-day event there should be consecutive days of long rides, aiming to cover about 30 miles one day followed by 20 the next at the speeds required in the forthcoming ride. During both days of the mock event watch out for any stable hints of stiffness, tiredness, or loss of appetite, as these are all indications of whether or not the horse is really fit.

The main difference between the one- and two-day competitive trail rides and the 100-mile-in-three-days rides is that the latter are a real test of durability, particularly on the third day when most dropouts occur.

On the first day a few horses will seize up, and during the second day's 40 miles a few more, but it is the third day's 20 miles which bring really fit horses to the fore and the border-line cases find it extremely difficult to summon up the free-going elastic stride of the competitive trail horse.

The shorter competitive trail rides can serve as an introduction to the 100 in three days for both horse and rider, but the rider should realize that not only is the distance almost doubled in the three-day rides, but that 40 miles of this distance still have to be covered after all pressure on the horse would have ceased in the shorter 40/20 rides. Conditioning, therefore, while following the same basic outline, will need to start earlier, with a very thorough lead-in period of slow work during which the horse gets used to carrying weight and being under the rider's direction for many hours at a stretch. It will be found that the horse that can apply himself and cooperate mentally as well as physically will be at an advantage. The horse that becomes overexcited or, at the other end of the scale, goes sour, is one that is not mentally prepared for the time stresses of competitive trail riding. Over the 100 miles the horse will be under saddle for approximately a 17-hour total, split 7, 7, and 3, and on top of that he will be under rider and veterinary restraint and supervision for about four hours a day. It takes a good horse with an equable disposition to be mentally alert yet relaxed, neither fretting nor turning sour, for such a long period of time, particularly in view of the fact that a horse's normal attention span is rather short.

If the horse is fit enough, your method of ride and stable care is properly thought out, and due attention has been paid to the mental side of preparing your horse, problems should not arise. Conditioning for long-distance riding should mean the horse is fit and willing enough to do more than the minimum he is asked for. If he can't or won't, he is either physically underconditioned or mentally unsuitable for competitive trail riding. The rider should aim to bring the horse in with virtually the same amount of elasticity in his stride and eagerness in his manner as at the ride start.

There are some problems more likely to crop up in the taxing 100-mile-in-three-days rides than in the shorter events. The horse's back may show signs of being slightly tender to the touch, which could cost you points (unless this is a normal condition, in which case it should be declared beforehand). You can alleviate back bruising by paying attention to the way you sit. This is one of the prime reasons for rising to the trot, because the rider is more comfortable and hence rides better, going with the horse rather than simply sitting on his back.

Legs may tend to fill overnight. This should not cause alarm if they are not feverish to the touch and the swelling subsides within a very short space of time after the resumption of work. Should the horse's legs be inclined to do this after resting up, it is an indication of a slight weakness. It may cost you points on the current ride but you will be forewarned for the next one. Veterinary advice should be obtained and any treatment suggested carried out. On one ride the veterinary judge found very slight heat and puffiness in Nizzolan's near fore check ligament. On veterinary advice I used a deep heat medication during training, discontinuing it prior to rides, and no further problems were encountered during competition. I lost two points on that ride, but being forewarned, I had no trouble the next time. Most horses have a weak spot somewhere and it takes a taxing competitive ride to find it out, because in ordinary hard work there are no judges to examine the horse systematically and objectively. A very slow buildup in early work is the best way to make sure that fever and filling do not occur during competition as this training will really strengthen the legs, tendons, and ligaments. However, working the horse too fast early in training will subject him to stresses that could well cause these point-costing symptoms in a horse that would normally be free of them. Most troubles really stem from injudicious or insufficient training early on, or from a program that started too late, with too much crammed into too short a time.

The second night of a 100-in-three-days competitive trail

ride is particularly revealing, as the horse will have covered 80 hard miles and if stress symptoms are going to show, in all probability they will crop up at this juncture. Some horses show relatively little stress en route, drawing on a reserve of energy while under saddle and only showing fatigue after work has ceased; it is back in stables that the true picture is often revealed. One sign to watch for is your horse's heart and respiration rates; another is any tendency to break into a cold sweat. This is indicative of either high tension or extreme fatigue. If the former, it will be accompanied by overly alert eyes, a keyed-up attitude, and heart and respiration rates which do not drop satisfactorily, and which tell you that the horse is not relaxing. If the cold sweat is accompanied by dull, lethargic eyes, it could mean excessive fatigue has set in. Many tired horses fail to clean up their grain satisfactorily—in fact just about the best indication of overall fitness in a competitive horse under actual ride conditions is that he is eating normally. This is one point where temperament plays a great part in the choice of the competitive horse, as the avid gourmet, whose chief delight is food regardless of his surroundings, will almost certainly be unaffected by eating under different conditions. His normal healthy appetite favors producing his energy requirements so that fatigue does not set in, and his preoccupation with his food shuts his mind to other conditions that could distract a tense animal.

If in-stable stress symptoms and fatigue show to any degree, very great care should be taken on the third and final lap of 20 miles, where you should aim merely to coast along. A tired horse can still be a sound horse and capable of finishing the ride, but should the rider push him over the top by demanding too much he may seize up completely. If he is coaxed along, he may well come in for a completion award. Each rider knows his own horse best and should know how to get the maximum out of him with the minimum effort on the horse's part. If this is not so, the rider has no business on a 100-miler and should stick to the less demanding events until he has acquired the necessary feel for fitness.

On 100-mile competitive trail rides no medications are allowed at any time and water may be used only at ordinary temperatures. This means that if problems crop up, no fast-acting remedy is permitted, as that would give the slightly failing horse an advantage over the supremely fit animal and placings would be affected unfairly.

It all comes down to early training and a constant alertness to possible weaknesses. This is one reason I am a firm believer in doing a miniride in my own territory a couple of weeks prior to the big event, so that there is still time to tighten up in various departments. All through training a watch should have been kept on the various stress sites such as back and legs. Another point to check is his dunging—a tired, overtaxed horse will scour, whereas a calm, fit horse's droppings will be normal. This is another reason for choosing a horse that has an equable temperament under stress conditions. Judges will impose penalties for constant scouring as it is extremely disadvantageous to a horse's general condition. On many competitive trail rides the horse's weight is taken by measuring him with a tape just behind the highpoint of the withers, and overall weight loss is taken into account when final placings are determined. The constantly scouring horse will suffer some dehydration and the energy expended on incessant scouring will debilitate him over-all. This in turn will have an adverse effect on his "taping" at the end of the ride. Horses, unlike people, seem to gain weight with difficulty and lose it easily.

Keep a careful eye on the horse's attitude during training. It helps to provide as much variety in his work as possible. Ride in company often; change your route as much as you can; vary the pace frequently. By that I do not mean that you should whittle him down below his proper weight by prolonged scampers, or upset his rhythm by chopping and changing gaits every minute or so, but if he is kept to an incessant walk or trot, he will become bored, particularly if going it alone. When a lively horse becomes bored he looks for excuses to misbehave; if a lazy horse is bored he virtually dies on you and is a worthless ride. If your horse is English-trained, you can vary the routine with the occasional spell of jumping. But I would not advise jumping too much as there is a risk of strain to tendons and the mistakes that so often occur in this sport could arrest your training. Although the next competitive trail ride may be months away, all your preparations will be wasted if your horse is laid up by a minor setback occasioned by, say, a bad landing, or a hard rap. A day at a local show, whether the horse is English- or western-trained, can give him an added interest in his work, particularly if it comes between the ride to and the journey back from the show. In the case of a working western horse his daily chores will keep him mentally fresh. I live in the New Forest, an open, wild area in the county of Hampshire, in the south of England, near Southampton. Here we can vary the horse's routine quite a bit with cattle drives and colt hunts. The cattle drives are steadily paced gatherings of the free-ranging cattle, which are brought into designated pounds for branding, taking to market, worming, or just moving to owners' private property. The colt hunts, when the year's crop of pony foals is rounded up for weaning, are very fast and involve exciting work in flushing foals and dams from their hiding places in the woods. Still do your mileage quota but vary it as much as possible and both horse and rider will stay fresh.

Training for Endurance Rides

THE next step up in long-distance riding is to the even more·
challenging true endurance ride. Although all long-distance-
ride training has the same basic requirements of careful
preparation over an extended period of time, sound horsemanship and horsemastership, good feeling, and an understanding
of the horse's mentality under pressure, endurance rides
definitely demand more from horse and rider in both physical
output and the application and expenditure of mental energy.
The horse will be subjected to a real test of endurance in
which he not only has to cover distance, but has to do so at
a greater consistent speed. In addition, for most of the endurance rides, particularly those over 50 miles, he will have
to keep up this accelerated performance for a much longer
time, especially if he is to achieve an award placing. Granted
most of these rides do have a lower required speed average
of 5 mph, but to achieve even this a higher rate of speed will
be needed for much of the time, as the nature of the terrain
in some parts of the route will force a drastic reduction in
speed.

In competitive trail rides, when the minimum and maximum times en route are laid down in the rules, the choice of
speed is very limited and all horses entered will be bearing
weight for approximately the same amount of time, the only
difference being the half-hour leeway for a 40-mile or a 15-
minute leeway for a 20-mile stint. In this type of riding the
rider should pay particular attention to a large number of stress
areas, which, broadly speaking, fall into three categories:

70/

1. Sustained speed.
2. The prolonged weight-bearing factor, especially in 50-mile-plus rides.
3. Extended mental strain.

In addition to appreciating the stress factors, you will have to satisfy yourself that the type of horse you own or have chosen is suited to this infinitely more demanding sphere of the sport. In a previous chapter, "Choosing the Endurance Horse," I covered the general aspects of choosing the competitive trail and/or endurance horse. Though endurance horses are ideally suited to tackling competitive trail riding the reverse is not necessarily true. The bulk of that chapter applies to selection of any good, long-distance trail horse, but endurance horses should have certain traits over and above those necessary for competitive trail mounts. Stresses in the areas just specified are much more intense for an endurance horse, and the field of suitable mounts narrows as the rides become longer and tougher. The actual physical makeup of the horse is more important than ever. I am not talking about conformation in the generally accepted sense, for the very good reason that a horse that has absolutely ideal conformation in terms of general and breed type concepts may not necessarily have the right conformation for endurance riding. In looking through results of endurance rides in the United States, Australia, and Great Britain, leaving out the matter of specific breeds, the type that is most successful is a small, compact, strong-boned, long-striding, wiry animal that would hardly win an accolade in a conformation class—although it is a pity that all show judges do not look for the structure beneath the show condition, as successful competitive horses in any phase of equestrian sport that entails a degree of stress must surely have a better conformation in real terms than pampered show arena beauties who don't know what work means.

The most suitable type of endurance horse carries no excess fat or heavy muscle, which does not mean he is lacking in condition or muscular development. On the contrary the ideal horse carries enough condition so he has that precious reserve needed for the stringent conditions he will meet, and his muscular development needs to be very good indeed, as great strength and elasticity without heaviness are vital. The heavy-boned and -muscled individual often combines his extra bulk with a heavier, less elastic way of going. This will tend to take more out of the horse, especially if he is asked for a continuous high speed, whereas the lighter framed and less fleshy horse has less bulk to cart around and usually has a lighter, more springy way of going; this means he tires himself and his rider less since his limbs, particularly the forehand, suffer less from concussion.

Once you are past the stage of deciding to tackle endurance riding proper and choosing a suitable mount, much of what goes for competitive trail riding still applies. Obviously you still need to put in the mileage, but now the horse should do a considerable amount of his training at a greater consistent speed. However, it is a mistake to concentrate on speed all the time. This exposes the horse to too much stress. You should take considerably longer to prepare for an endurance ride than for a competitive trail ride. This applies particularly to the longer rides, but whether aiming for a 50-miler or a 100-miler, I should want to pay more attention to the initial stages of very slow work than I would for a competitive trail ride, as this slow buildup is the strong rock on which to build and on which the horse is going to rely when he is asked for peak performance. In endurance riding even more than in other forms of long-distance riding, too hurried a preparation will almost certainly mean a physical breakdown in actual competition, if not sooner, during training. If a rider should be lucky enough to get away with insufficient preparation once, it is no guarantee that he will continue to do so. The strain is that much greater in endurance than in competitive trail riding, so preparation should be that much more careful, for if a breakdown due to insufficient preparation occurs in endurance riding it is likely to be of a much more serious nature, with more far-reaching effects in regard to future usefulness.

Ideally those tackling endurance riding should do so as a progression from competitive trail riding. They will already have gained invaluable experience in many of the areas they will continue to meet in endurance riding and have tested the suitability of their mount under actual ride conditions, both en route and back at ride base. They will also have learned those subtle nuances of mood and performance that indicate how their horse feels and how much drive and reserve he has left. Following the principle of moving steadily upward in type of competition, they would be wise to tackle a 50-miler first.

In endurance riding the fastest fit horse across the finish line is the winner; the rides have a maximum time in which horses must finish to qualify for a completion award, ranging from a 50 in 10 hours (some rides have 12 hours as the outside time) to a 100 in 24 hours. However, this time is total elapsed time, out of which must come the compulsory veterinary checks and rest periods, so the total ridden time is somewhat less, varying with the specific regulations for each ride; winning times are always taken on the total ridden time, so that to be up among the leaders of a 50-miler you will need to average around 10 mph—almost 50 percent faster than for competitive trail riding. If you try going much over that speed it will only result in disaster for the horse, as he will burn himself out far too quickly and in all likelihood fail to pass one of the veterinary checks and not be allowed to proceed.

You should take a good three months to prepare properly for a 50-mile endurance ride, assuming the horse is already fit for light work. During the first five weeks follow the training schedule set out for competitive trail riding. In the sixth week tighten up by gradually lengthening the distances traveled, but without increasing the speed. About the eighth week the real distance workouts should begin, stepping up from 25 and 30 miles to 40 miles at a go, till 40 miles is a jaunt, and in the last month the speed workouts should begin, building from 10 miles in an hour. This distance should be incorporated into a regular day's workout of 20 to 25 miles. However, do not make the mistake of constantly doing prolonged rides or speed workouts. Too many of these result in a horse with a drawn physique and nervous disposition, always fretting to go instead of relaxing into his stride.

The horse's normal working week will be five to six days, depending on his attitude. If he is a little jaded give him two consecutive days off. After you have started on the real distances, but before the speed workouts begin, make three of the six working days long-ride days, aiming at distances between 20 and 30 miles. As you go into the last month when the speed element is added and distances are increasing, two distance workouts a week would be sufficient, with one of them extended to between 35 and 40 miles. However, one of the nondistance days should be a sprint workout, so that three of the six working days will involve high energy expenditure and the other three normal work, with at least one of these a really easy day so that the horse does not always expect to be pushed to his limit.

This is not intended as a rigid program, as experience and feel for your own particular mount will be your best guide, and not all horses respond in the same way. In other words, while using common sense and keeping the relevant requirements of speed and distance in mind, gradually tighten up on both as training progresses. A watch must be kept to strike the balance between getting the horse fit, keeping him keen, and allowing sufficient rest and relaxation. This is not easy and, unless you are a genius, you will make mistakes from time to time over the years. You can learn from your mistakes and being forewarned will help to make these minor errors, not the major ones that cause lengthy setbacks in your planned program.

I frequently do some of my speed training on my way to the farrier, who lives across eleven miles of open forest and moorland. When calling for high speed performance I aim to do this distance in fractionally over the hour, have the horse shod, and return at the same speed. I find this a very good tryout particularly as, depending on rainfall, the footing varies from holding to firm, stony to good, with a little roadwork as well. The horse learns to cope at speed with different ground conditions by remaining alert, and as soon as he realizes he is on a workout he gives no trouble fooling around. When fit, the horses do not become distressed, and within minutes after the hard riding stops, their breathing is normal; the walk in for the last part of the journey suffices both to cool the hide and to allow heart and respiratory recovery. An added advantage of doing a speed workout, or any other type of conditioning, this way is that riding with an objective is far more interesting than merely putting in the allotted distance with added mileage as your sole reason.

Commence your speed workouts during the last four to five weeks and increase the distances gradually. Occasionally limit yourself to a sprint ride of approximately an hour, allowing cooling out time, of course, in the last mile or so. As the time for the ride approaches, it is wise to do a simulated endurance ride, aiming for approximately 35 to 40 miles done at an average of 10 mph. There should, of course, be a layover of approximately an hour at the 20-mile mark to assess recovery rates and satisfy yourself the horse is fit to proceed. In other words aim for simulated ride conditions. If you are going for a placing speed, the long-distance trial should be done a minimum of ten days, preferably two weeks, before the event. Going for the higher speed will put more of a strain on the horse, so spacing two very fast, long rides too close together is not wise. After this, training should revert to normal for the penultimate week, followed by the final week when work should ease considerably, allowing two nonconsecutive days off, one of which will be the horse's traveling day to the ride. Then he gets to the event really fit and eager, not overworked and past his fighting best.

A rough guide to a final week's work when the horse should be kept ticking over, but not pressed hard, would be (assuming that the event is on a Saturday):

Sunday. Two to three hours of steady work with the accent on relaxed performance.
Monday. The same type of work but not more than two hours.
Tuesday. Rest day.
Wednesday. The last day of real work, with a 30-mile sharpish ride.
Thursday. Travel day, and the horse should simply be walked and trotted slowly for about 30 minutes to an hour after he has settled in. This is considered a rest day and the

walking/trotting is to ease any travel stiffness; also, at the base stable he has no pasture to roam in as he did at home.

Friday. About an hour to an hour and a half of very easy work, just to let him limber up and settle into new surroundings. Later in the day he should be walked in hand for 15 to 20 minutes.

During this final phase of training you will get a clearer idea of whether your horse is really suited to the high-speed-plus-distance events. However suitable a horse may seem, it is only in actual practice that his owner can measure his true capabilities and in the light of this knowledge decide whether to aim for completion only, or to try for a place, as the latter means achieving a consistent high average throughout the 50, 75, or 100 miles. It is an extreme test of a horse, and past history has shown that most successful horses have been of the type described earlier. When the chips are down it is not the very fast animal but the one who has endless stamina allied with a fair speed that comes out on top. It takes real grit and determination to keep up a relentless speed of 8 to 10 mph over ground that is chosen because it is testing and exacts a horse's maximum performance. No unfit horse, or one with structural inadequacies, will ever cover 50 miles at approximately 10 mph and finish ready for more. Even less will he finish the longer, tougher rides which are the natural progression if the rider feels his horse has the iron constitution, and he himself has the dedication, that the longest rides demand.

As distances increase to the 75-mile and then to the 100-mile acme of endurance riding, all the points covered in the preceding pages relating to conditioning still obtain: stress, accelerated performance, consistency of speed, rating of the horse, ability to bear weight; and as the demands are intensified, the margins for slight deviations from the ideal are narrowed.

It calls for real dedication and supreme fitness from both horse and rider to embark on the stringent routine needed to successfully complete these exceptionally tough rides. Previously, while covering long-distance riding in general and the less-demanding spheres of competitive trail riding. I have said that it is not absolutely imperative to stick to a rigid routine, but rather to aim at maintaining a workable skeleton schedule. However, as work and stresses increase and the leeway for error lessens, the routine must become tighter, and training sessions now take on the dimensions of previous actual rides. You will have left it too late in the day if you wait till the ride itself to find out whether your mount can really do the distance coupled with the speed, and although it is not necessary to cover identical mileage on training trips, you should include an approximation several times in your training schedule, so that during the last five weeks of training for a 75-miler there would be a minimum of two stints of 50 to 60 miles, spaced far enough apart, with the last and longest trial taking place a minimum of ten days before the actual ride. The general rule of not asking too much too close to the ride and not souring or overtaxing the horse still applies. Continued excessive demands are the finest way to debilitate a horse in mind and body, particularly in the all-important leg region, where most breakdowns occur.

It is not necessary to do all these lengthy training trips at competition speed, but it would be wise to try for at least one, preferably the last, under simulated ride conditions, spacing the hour-long halts at intervals throughout the mileage and giving the horse the same care that he will receive under ride conditions.

Much of the ride training is dictated by common sense, coupled with meticulous attention to detail and an extreme awareness of every slight nuance in the horse's moods and physical output. For instance, if the horse is slightly fatigued and his way of going becomes rather heavy or dragging, or if he seems jaded on a comparatively short ride, it may just mean he needs a little more incentive, such as the company of another horse, or a short breather, before going on and finding his competitive spirit again. No great harm will be done if he continues on course, as the fatigue will only be superficial if he has been properly conditioned. However, should the horse show a similar lack of drive under greater stress the symptoms probably go deeper, and pushing on at a critical phase could be damaging, whereas relaxing drive and speed will give the horse time to recover his energy and refresh his mind for a further surge forward. Under these conditions it is absolutely vital that the rider know every facet of his mount's makeup, and for best results not only should the rider do all the horse's training, but he should also take complete care of him in the stable. It is the only way to really understand the horse.

For the 100s much the same principles apply as already outlined for the two lower endurance categories and, I must reiterate, the limits in which mistakes can occur in training and be rectified satisfactorily are even narrower. Bear in mind that as distances lengthen the horse will have less and less reserve left, and greater care will be needed to conserve energy for the latter part of the course. Also the weight-bearing factor is at its most important at this distance. In the other rides the time under saddle could approximate a really long day's work in other spheres, such as hunting, where it is quite common to be aboard for six to eight hours at a stretch if one hacks to the meet, or ranch work, where the horse is daily worked hard. However, in the 100s time under saddle will range from a minimum of around 12 hours to the maximum permitted, around 20 hours. The very fact of bearing weight for this time is going to take a toll on the horse, and going slowly to conserve energy is somewhat balanced by the extra energy needed to bear weight for the added time. This is one very good reason to do several miniendurance rides, in which the rider appraises his horse's capabilities with this weight-bearing factor to the fore.

To go back to the question of energy reserves, I can illustrate from my own experience with Nizzolan and his Golden Horseshoes. In these competitions a horse has to travel at a minimum average of 9 mph if he is to be in for the top award of a Gold. He must also acquire full veterinary marks— one single point lost in that department means he goes down to the next category of a Silver. When aiming for Gold I find that during the first few miles Nizzolan is settling into a mental and physical rhythm while he makes up his mind as to the intensity of ride demands. After the first few miles he always seems to realize what it is going to be—endurance or competitive trail—and gears his mood and gait accordingly. Once he has this sorted in his own mind his drive on the first 25 miles is of adequate proportions; on the second 25 miles he has plenty of reserve left but may tend to drop a notch or two in ebullience around the 50-mile mark, racking up more verve in the last 5 miles of the 50-mile session. On the first part of the third and final lap of 25 miles he will not show much enthusiasm, but once the first ten miles of that are behind him he really picks up, and at the end of the 75 miles he is going much stronger than he was at the end of 50. The average properly conditioned endurance horse shows a pattern to energy production which could broadly be set out as: settling into rhythm at ride start, followed by a level plane of performance for the bulk of the ride with a slight drop in energy toward the two-thirds mark, followed by a gradual pickup and, if the horse is not pushed too much during this phase, a real boost toward and right up to the end of the ride. A horse that can follow this pattern is of the right stamp and also has been conditioned according to ride requirements.

During training, and particularly on the really long trips, the rider should pay particular attention to this evolving pattern; he will find that the horse's performance will teach him a tremendous amount, offering either incentive to go on to more stringent demands or a warning to drop back to a less punishing routine. It would be very wise to aim only for completion on your first few endurance rides, using them to get to know the horse in competition as well as in training before going on to ask for the supreme effort needed to be up in the rankings.

For a 50-mile endurance ride the average ranking or placing speeds are between 9 and 10 mph, and the completion speeds at the lower end of the scale can average around 5 mph. For 100-mile-in-one-day events, placing speeds average around 8 mph or a little over for the winner and top two or three, but 6 to 7 mph for the minor placings, with the lower-scale completion speeds about 5 mph, as for the 50. This does not mean that all 100s are won by the 8-mph horses. Both the condition of the route and the quality of the horses vary and winning time can be considerably lower, but these times are frequently turned in at the peak events.

During the three-month training period for the 50-miler, the long rides are entered into around the sixth week, and the even more extended mileages around the eighth week. The same schedule can be followed for the longer 75- and 100-mile rides as regards distance, but the speed should not be so accelerated. This is because the eighth week of 50-mile training is nearing the end of the road as far as that competition is concerned, but the eighth week in 75- or 100-mile training is still relatively close to the beginning, and slow buildup is absolutely essential. This means that, while it takes about three months to prepare for a 50-miler, you should add another six weeks to two months for a 75-miler and a further two months on top of that for a 100-miler. All these times assume that the horse is already in light work, not straight off a lush pasture and pig-fat, nor in a state that needs considerable condition added before he can go into training. Throughout conditioning minirests should be given to maintain eagerness and verve.

Heat is something I have not yet mentioned in connection with either competitive trail riding or endurance riding. In Britain we do not have to contend with this to any great degree, although on many rides in England I have heard competitors complaining of the heat when to me it has seemed only pleasantly warm. What they would do in America I do not know. I do think though that the general type of horse that competes in Britain, with the exception of the Arab, part-Arab, and Thoroughbred, would find it very difficult to cope with the heat conditions prevalent in the United States.

Heat poses several problems that can affect the horse's performance deleteriously, the most obvious one being that of dehydration and loss of essential salts in the system. If severe, this could cause the horse to suffer cramps and colic. It can also cause a horse's muscles to tie up so that he will be in considerable distress and cannot proceed. It is most important, therefore, to take precautions by seeing that the horse has access to salt with his normal rations and, if excess energy expenditure is expected, by adding extra salt to his rations a day or so prior to the ride. Do not add so much that he will retain an inordinately large amount of fluid, as this in itself can cause more stress than his system can endure under ride conditions. I add salt to feed by dampening the feed with liquidized mineral salts. I usually do this two days before a ride, as it then has time to get into the system (the digestive tract is slow-moving, any intake needing many hours to be thoroughly absorbed, though some foods are absorbed more readily than others). Some horses do not relish this addition to their feed, so try your own horse with it well in advance so that it does not come as "something different" so late in the training.

Some horses sweat profusely, some moderately, some hardly at all, even under pressure. Find out what is natural for your particular horse and use this as a guide to salt loss, remembering that all horses lose some essential salts during hard work, both in normal bodily processes and through sweat. I will deal with this salt factor more fully in the feeding and care chapters.

Heat also affects the degree of fatigue. Many riders try to train in the cool of the morning or evening. This is fine while the horse is being brought slowly into work, but if he is to be fit for any and all conditions—and rides are run in just about all kinds of weather—he must get used to working at full stretch in all weather conditions. If he has a chance to get used to heat in training, he will be able to take it in his stride much better during the ride than if he meets with it for the first time on the day itself. On cool days, which often have a freshening breeze as well, the horse will work with that much more zip, and the weather will be reflected in his general condition in terms of energy reserve and heart and respiration rates. Extreme heat will impose more of a strain and a watch will have to be kept on the horse for stress in these areas. Should heart and respiration become labored, pace must be considerably eased until the horse has recovered to as close to normal as possible. Extreme fatigue will also bring on excessive sweating. Normal to heavy sweating in humid weather is good, but a laboring horse that sweats to excess is in danger of dehydration. Maintaining the right fluid balance is a very important aspect of endurance and/or competitive trail ride preparation, and paying attention to the amount and degree of saltiness of the sweat, general appearance of the horse before and after an arduous workout, and manner of work under different heat conditions during training will help the rider avert the problems that excessive heat can cause. Obviously heat will have more of an effect on an already tiring horse, so the middle section of an endurance ride, which probably takes place during the hottest part of the day when the horse is beginning to feel the first signs of weariness, should be ridden with extreme care. Fluid balance is also dealt with in later chapters on care before, during, and after the ride itself.

This and the preceding chapter on training have been written mainly for the rider who is thinking of entering only one or two rides. Obviously some riders would like to plan a whole season of competitive events, and in that case, whether one is aiming for competitive trail or endurance riding, other points become relevant. Instead of gearing your horse toward one event, with training specifically detailed for that particular ride, other factors have to be taken into account. There may be long gaps between events, thereby drawing the conditioning out for too long a period. In this event it is as well to give the horse a short holiday. This will benefit him mentally and give him a chance to ease up physically. Also leg problems will be a more likely hazard if training is nonstop than if a horse is partially let down from time to time. Having already proved that the horse can take the strain of competitive trail and/or endurance riding, and having yourself gained considerable experience over the time already spent training him, you will know how much time is needed to bring him back to peak performance. If the letdown period is to last from two weeks to a month, put him onto good grass, but do not completely turn him away onto rich grazing, or he will blow up and be correspondingly more difficult to recondition. Also there will be the risk of laminitis (hoof founder). I would advise putting him out during the day and bringing him in at night if it is cool, reversing the procedure if it is hot. Keep a little hard feed in his diet—about 5 pounds a day, with enough hay so he does not get too soft or bored while in the stable.

Apart from this short holiday, care should be taken throughout training that the horse does not become stale through overwork and boredom. If you feel his responses are a little sluggish, his work rather dull and automatic, or his general attitude not as bright as usual, it may be he needs a minibreak of three or four days. This will not affect his training to any great extent, and what is lost in mileage covered will be more than made up for by extra vitality.

With more long-distance, competitive, and endurance rides coming into the equestrian calendar each year, some riders may like to consider how to keep the horse in training for a whole season, possibly with a first ride in March and a final one at the end of October. That means an eight-month competitive season, with several months' conditioning before the first event. This takes a really fit horse who relishes work and maintains a fresh, gay outlook all the time.

Fresh is the key word when you are putting a horse into a whole season's competitive riding. I like to bring him to the start of training after a two- to three-month layoff, when the most that has been asked of him is a light hack once in a while to prevent his getting bored. This is important, particularly for an active horse who is not used to being idle. After such a rest from the previous year's rides and general work, he comes back into work in an eager, keen manner.

With approximately ten months of work ahead of him before his next complete rest, it is important for the rider to work out in advance exactly what he intends to do with the horse. Decide on which rides (and other events, if he is a versatile performer) you will be entering and space them so that he will never be taxed beyond his limit. Just because a horse finishes a hard event in fine fettle does not mean he should be taken advantage of and pushed into successive events too close together. If you do this, he runs the risk of overworking his frame to the extent that he will eventually not be able to bounce back to peak condition, but will have to have a long rest to recover.

In working out his program decide which are going to be your high spots of the year and plan your training around them. If between the big rides there are minor ones, or long-distance pleasure rides, use these as additional training rides which will give the horse a change from routine.

Because you will be keeping the horse hard, fit, and ready for competition for eight consecutive months, he should not be pushed to excessive speed in his training or asked to do too many distance workouts. After the first long-distance ride of the season, he will be entering enough competitive and pleasure events to have those substituted for his distance and speed workouts. Once you know your animal's capabilities there is no need to constantly try him out. Do not take this to mean that long rides can be cut out of the interim training completely. The foregoing is meant as a guide and a warning not to overdo the mileage. Over this long period there should be several minibreaks for freshening the horse, preferably after a competitive ride. A rough guide could be obtained from how I planned two of my Golden Horseshoe entries in 1973.

I entered Nizzolan and Katchina in a 40-mile May Qualifier at Goodwood, so their real training started in early April and their program went like this.

End of April. 20-plus-mile pleasure ride over flat New Forest terrain.

May 20th. Goodwood, 40-miler over fairly hilly country (averaging just over 7 mph).

One week off. Easing back into work over the next two. Nizzolan, because he was standing at stud, had his work programmed slightly differently from Katchina's, with allowance made for energies expended at stud.

June and July. Steady progression toward another Qualifier, this one to be done at speed.

July 28th. 42-miler at an average speed of 8½ mph, followed by a minibreak of around a week with only very light hacking.

August 20th. A 23-mile pleasure ride in Gloucestershire done at 7½ mph. (Only Nizzolan took part in this as the other side of the trailer was taken up by a friend's horse.)

September 6th, 7th, 8th. Golden Horseshoe at Cheltenham in the Cotswold Hills in Gloucestershire for both. Time includes day before for vetting, etc. Very tough gradients, and very humid conditions. Nizzolan a Gold, averaging 9.4 on first 50, and 9.6 on last 25. Katchina a Silver.

Then one week's loafing for both of them, followed by two weeks during which Nizzolan was brought back to a ticking-over fitness with only a couple of really long rides of about 20 plus miles.

September 29th. Endurance Horse and Pony Society Competitive Trail 40-plus-miler at Beaulieu Abbey, in Hampshire. That finished Nizzolan's year, but Katchina was then brought back to peak performance for his final ride of the year in Devon over rolling moorland with reasonable gradients.

October 20th. Endurance Horse and Pony Society Competitive Trail 35-miler at Postbridge, Devon.

Both these horses were then roughed off for a complete rest and eased back into work about the end of January, with no serious training until early March, ready for the next season.

During more intensive training, when I felt the horses were becoming just a little stale (particularly Nizzolan, who had taken more work than Katchina because of fox-hunting during the winter), they had the occasional two-day break instead of one day a week off.

This system worked well for both horses. Nizzolan, then 6 years old, is a purebred Arab stallion of the spare-framed type, standing 15 hands and weighing approximately 950 pounds. Katchina, then 5 years old, is heavier in bone, but also in spare condition, standing 14.1½ and weighing approximately 900 pounds. Although in lean, fit condition neither horse ran up light after competition, what minimal weight loss they may have sustained was replaced with a maximum of two days, and, in fact, from May onward both gained considerably, which proved the work suited them. At no time during their rides was either horse pushed to his limit, both having plenty of reserve left for that bit extra should it have been needed.

When you are training for an extended season, distance workouts have to be thought of as part of a whole season's work, not just preparation for one specific ride, which is the reason some of the actual competitions should be substituted for long-distance workouts. Naturally these will be timed somewhat differently to a one-ride training schedule, but it is up to the rider to study at the beginning of the season the mileages of these events and the types of country they will be run over and plan a rough work chart for the season so that he can then add or subtract his training workouts from the sum total. In this way he can arrive at the ideal work load for his endurance horse.

The following year, 1974, for Nizzolan went like this:

April 7th. 40-mile Qualifier at minimum 7 mph, Somerset— very tough going.

April 20th. 20-mile pleasure ride over New Forest, Hampshire —fairly flat going.

May 5th. 20-mile pleasure ride done at 8½ mph; used as a training ride for:

May 16/18th. Golden Horseshoe Ride, Taunton, Somerset— again hills and tough going (Gold award).

June 22nd. 18-mile pleasure ride, Ashdown Forest, undulating going.

July 27th. 40-mile competitive trail ride, Surrey—very mixed going: some level, some hills, some holding sand, some roadwork.

September 8th. 20-mile pleasure ride, New Forest.

September 14th. 50-mile competitive trail ride, New Forest.

October 5th. 40-mile competitive trail ride, Devon—very severe going.

October 26th. 20-mile pleasure ride, New Forest.

Finally, two months' holiday in preparation for training for 1975 with its highspots of Golden Horseshoe 75 Miles Endurance, and New Forest 100 Mile in 24 Hours Endurance.

Horse Care and Ride Tactics

CARE of the endurance horse is largely a matter of keeping him relaxed and adaptable. Make sure he has a sensible feeding routine, generally regular without being rigid—that is, don't feed him at 6 A.M. one day and 10 A.M. the next. Minor variations in feeding time are quite all right—in fact, if the horse expects his oats precisely on the dot each day he may also start acquiring aggravating habits such as pawing or fidgetiness if he isn't appeased with his bucket.

Throughout training I give my horses pasture freedom for most of the day, bringing them in at night. In summer I can reverse this in the bad fly season except with the stallion Nizzolan, since I live close to the New Forest where there are free-ranging stallions and I don't much like the idea of his arguing with Forest stallions or hopping the fence to visit the free-roaming mare bands. Magnet also has to be stabled at night as occasionally she jumps out. She doesn't go anywhere, but the resulting repair work is more aggravating than an extra box to clean.

My own fields do not produce good grass and I do not own enough acreage to provide proper feed, so it is safe to let the horses be out without restriction. However, if the pasture is lush, grazing must be reduced. A horse that really bloats must be severely restricted, and a bare, or almost bare, paddock provided for his roamings.

Try to provide a companion when the horse is out, as he will be more settled in company. Frequently horses turned out alone, particularly those with a nervous temperament, take to fence walking, which whittles their condition and shows they are far from relaxed mentally. It is important for his overall well-being that the horse should have a certain amount of freedom, as he will be much more relaxed and better settled in his ridden work. For a horse in endurance training it is a good method of keeping him free from muscular stiffness, as he continually moves gently around when grazing, whereas confinement means he is forced into inactivity. It is certainly worth the bit of extra trouble getting the dirt out of his coat.

Grooming should be thorough, especially where tack touches the skin. A chafe on an endurance horse is more serious than one on an animal used for ordinary riding, as it may mean cessation of training at a vital point. Saddle pads should be washed frequently, or, if they are the hard-to-wash western variety, they should be well dried and the dirt beaten out with a stick.

If the horse has a heavy coat, clip him even in summer. It will be easier to keep flesh on him, as clammy hair acts like a Turkish bath when he is hot and is a surefire chiller when cold, pulling condition off him either way. However, when clipping, leave hair around the fetlocks as an added guard against scratches, and leave a band of hair under the girth as well as a saddle patch, as these areas need extra protection.

If you are entering any rides which mean being away from home stabling for a few days, try to arrange a trial period away to see the horse's reactions. I have a friend whose horse refused food on one Golden Horseshoe because he was away from home and separated from his normal companions; this resulted in distress and later on in colic and withdrawal from the ride. Now my friend thinks ahead, accustoming the horse to nights away in different places, so that he has become more settled in strange surroundings.

You may find that the horse goes off his feed and water the first time or two away from home, so it is well worth the added expense to do a couple of these away-from-home sessions in the first year of competition so that at an actual event the horse does not face this additional stress. If you skimp on these trial sessions with a horse known to be distressed in strange surroundings, you are really wasting the time, effort, and expenditure that goes into producing the endurance horse; where you might have gained a high placing award with a mentally relaxed mount, the horse may only come in with a completion rosette, or have to be withdrawn altogether if he is too upset.

When a horse is relaxed he will eat. Water is another thing, and it is more vital than food on an endurance ride. A horse can draw on his flesh reserves as a substitute for food, but dehydration may put him in a really bad way and result in his being withdrawn by a vet. If this is a known problem, it is sometimes possible to get around it by adding a smidgen of wintergreen to his water at home for a few days prior to traveling so that he will become used to it. Then, with the same flavor addition to his water in strange stables, he will not notice any change. Alternatively, you can take water in a container if you are going only for one night, but this is very impractical for longer periods. However, the much-traveled horse soon learns to accept what he is offered in the way of water and accommodation.

Nizzolan is reluctant to drink strange water at first, but by the next day he has settled down to accepting what is offered. Consequently I always try to get to the ride the day before, if it is a one-day event, and for the Golden Horseshoe I like to arrive on Wednesday for a Friday start. Katchina and Magnet Regent offer no problems, drinking and eating whatever comes their way.

Prior to packing for my trips away from home I make lists and check off items as they are loaded. All feed and hay should be taken, as sudden changes in diet can be disastrous. Allow extra in case the return is delayed. I also take a jar of loose iodized salt, regular grooming kit, shovel and fork, a spare set of shoes for the horse, a spare hoof pick to tie on the saddle, a rasp for beveling sharp edges that wear on his shoes, at least three clean saddle pads plus his exercise one, a light blanket and two coolers (in case it is raining and one gets wet at a midway check), two spare girths, a needle and strong thread for quick repairs and also for braiding the horse's tail to hock length if it should be very muddy, since it is uncomfortable for him to have it clinging wetly around his hind legs, tack-cleaning gear, insect repellant, extra buckets, a water container, an antiseptic spray, wound ointment, and antiseptic dusting powder in case a chafe occurs. With these latter items it is wise to check ride rules, as some rides forbid use of any medications, internal or external, immediately prior to and during the ride.

As far as my own equipment goes, I pack a complete change of everything because of the unpredictability of the weather. In addition I pack a pair of light shoes with soles suitable for gripping slippery surfaces. I have found I can make better time on foot than riding if I lead the horse at a run over slick patches, or down slippery blacktopped roads that would mean walking if I remain mounted. The horse is better balanced and less liable to slip without my weight on his back. Shoes may not look as good as proper boots, but the end result is more important than a model turnout. You should check ride rules thoroughly regarding dismounting and leading en route, as some rides, usually the endurance ones, permit this, and others, usually the competitive trail rides, do not.

By all means be neat, but be practical as well. I am more comfortable in a sweater and loose jeans than in jodhpurs and jacket. However, at award presentations do dress appropriately, as the rider should do credit to a horse that has worked well for him. Gloves can be very necessary in case weather should turn wet and make reins slippery. Also on bitterly cold days fingers stiffen and it is not easy to handle reins with frozen hands, particularly if your horse needs a fairly strong contact. Leather chaps afford considerable grip and are very comfortable and warm as well as providing a certain amount of weatherproofing.

Insect repellent is useful for both horse and rider. Wiped on the horse's face it will keep the flies from bothering him.

I think it most necessary to have the horse at ride base at least the day before an event, earlier if feasible. It gives him a chance to settle into new surroundings and get over any trailer weariness; also, if his legs have filled in traveling, there will be time for this to sort itself out. Arriving early has the advantage of getting the rider settled as well, and this is important, as any tension in the rider will be communicated to the horse, who will begin thinking tension is part of the whole scene.

If your horse is a bed eater, request some bedding other than straw when booking accommodation. Most organizers make provision for this. If not, be prepared to carry a bale of shavings, sawdust, or peat with you as part of your ride equipment; otherwise a horse can stuff himself so much the night before that it adversely affects his ride performance. If the sawdust or peat is very dry, slightly dampen it by sprinkling water on top, or it may make the horse cough.

Stallion owners should be aware that some organizers prefer putting all stallions in one stable section. I do not think this is fair to those who are used to their own companions and are well behaved. I have always found ride organizers most cooperative when I request Nizzolan be stabled with his traveling companion, nearly always one of his own stablemates or a horse with whom he trains. However, if a stallion should upset those next door to him, the ride organizer has every right, in the interest of other horses' tranquillity, to move him to more appropriate surroundings.

When your horse is in his temporary surroundings don't keep fussing around him with brushes, etc. Attend to him normally and let him alone. Just the fact that you are there is reassuring. I have noticed that horses coming to my stable to be boarded and/or trained are sometimes ill at ease at first because, particularly in the case of much-traveled ones, they never seem to realize where they truly belong. My own animals, particularly Nizzolan and Magnet, have been very widely traveled. Magnet competed in the States and then had several different homes in Britain till I found a place to buy. Nizzolan was in North Carolina till a year old, and then also went through several changes in Britain, plus three seasons of heavy competition in long-distance rides. Neither of these horses has ever been worried by the changes, I think, because the one constant has been that I have always been with them. So it is as much who they are with as where they are that means home to a horse.

Many ride organizers have a list of stables where horses

can be accommodated prior to a ride if you wish to be really early and finish up your training on the spot. It is a good idea to carry a claw hammer and a few nails with you. I always make a routine check of any box I put a horse into and immediately remove any projecting nails. It is really amazing how many stables, even first-rate ones, have a number of these and get away without injury to their own horses.

Another point: there should be no gap between wall and floor in which a horse can trap a hoof when rolling. If there is, tactfully ask for a board to be fixed there temporarily, even if you have to say your horse is prone to damaging himself. If the hay ring is too low don't use it. Waste some hay for once and feed off the floor rather than risk a hung hoof. Alternatively make your own hay ring. I do this by plaiting strands of twine from the hay bales and running the result over a rafter. Being tall I can reach up and snap a net to this, and when empty the net is still several feet clear of the floor and safe for the horse.

You should spend the night as close to the ride stables as possible, and if the riders' accommodation is not in the immediate vicinity leave your name, where you are staying, and the telephone number with the ride's stable manager.

All events have preride veterinary checks. Make sure you declare any peculiarities in gait or elsewhere. If these are noted on the horse's scorecard, they will not be held against him during the competition unless they impede his performance. For instance, declare such things as windgalls, touchy back, a hitch in gait not due to lameness, fresh cuts or bruises he may have prior to the ride that could be in a significant place, such as an interference mark on legs or hooves, tendency to sweat very freely (some horses are excessive sweaters even when fit). Sometimes a vet will find things you didn't even know were there which can help with future declarations or preride precautions. One point especially for those who have done several rides already or whose memories occasionally let them down: sometimes such things as windgalls are permanent. They do the horse no harm unless they harden, and very few horses that have really worked are without them to some degree or other. One gets so used to them, and considers them so harmless, that one is inclined to forget to declare them at ride start—I know, because I have made this mistake and received a small penalty at the end of the ride. Therefore I try to make a point of making out a card beforehand detailing all the odds and ends that need to be declared.

When reading the ride schedule, take special note of any warnings about the route. Even if no warnings are given, it is best to stick carefully to the marked track, as the course setters know the terrain best.

I illustrate with two incidents in England which must surely have parallels in America:

A competitor on a New Forest Qualifier which I organized deviated from the marked route by a fraction and her horse went into a Forest bog up to his belly. The horse heaved himself clear, but the rider was mired to her waist and too frightened to move. Fortunately another competitor riding a Western-trained horse came along with a lariat and roped the lady out of the bog.

The other, more frightening, incident was when a party of riders touring horseback in Wales went off the safe route and found themselves sinking whichever way they turned. The area was remote, and they had to spend a whole night holding their horses until they were rescued by search parties sent out the next morning.

All ride routes are checked and it is safe to follow the indicated path though it may be a bit cut up in places. Even then, however, you should keep your eyes open as markers are sometimes shifted by pranksters. If you notice sudden lush green amid dry surroundings, it probably means bog. In areas where there is scrub, sedge, cattail, reeds, or tussock grass, there is swamp and the footing is unsafe. Unsafe patches sometimes appear in the middle of a hillside, indicated by sharply contrasting bright growth against the drier fern and heather or scrub. The fact that you are on a hill is no indication of dryness. Often the structure of the subsoil changes abruptly, causing dangerous pockets of mire. Clay is another hazard. If you suddenly notice thick yellow clay, go slowly. Its holding qualities suffice to drag a horse down or cause a somersault, particularly if ridden into at speed. Some terrain has an odd tendency to change from time to time; what may be perfectly safe one year may develop tricky pockets later on, and really knowing your territory takes time. These warnings may seem odd coming from someone who now lives and rides in England, but when I first came to the New Forest to live, after spending nearly nine years in North Carolina, I was struck by many similarities between the danger spots in the Forest and the type I was used to in the Coastal Plain of North Carolina.

However, there is no great cause for alarm as the rides are carefully routed and normally take place in the drier seasons of the year when these hazards, apart from never-drying bogs, are minimal.

Gravelly streams are safe. Streams that are not clear and have a very cut-up approach may not be safe for a horse with the added weight of a rider aboard.

On ride day I like to feed the horse very early, about three hours before my scheduled start. Then just about an hour before the start I like to offer a tiny feed of about 1 pound. Groom thoroughly and saddle up very carefully, paying particular attention to placing the saddle pad, if used, and to the girth, making sure there are no skin wrinkles that could chafe.

I carry a piece of string in my pocket; a hoof pick on the saddle, or in my pocket if that particular saddle has no dees at the back; a small sponge or cloth for wiping the horse's face (if you have a backup team to help, they can provide this at stops en route); a twist of paper in which there is some antiseptic powder if the ride rules permit medications during the event (competitive trail ride rules in the United States do not). I also carry a clean handkerchief and bandage in case of an emergency. Then any bleeding can be stopped and if necessary a temporary bandage applied. I know this sounds like a lot to carry in pockets, but in fact it takes very little space if packed efficiently.

Prior to starting in the morning I pack everything I need in my Landrover (the British substitute for a Jeep or pickup truck), parking it where I can get to it at mid-ride check if this is to be at ride base, or getting a friend to drive it to the scheduled stops. The list of things needed includes: two water buckets; a container of hot water, so that it will still have the chill off by the time it is offered to the horse (on competitive trail rides with their rules regarding water at "ordinary temperature only," or if it is obviously going to be a hot day, place the container in a position where the sun can warm the water); a light blanket; his cooler sheet (I have a lightweight wool one for cold weather, and a close-mesh cotton one for hot days); large sponges; dandy brush; antiseptic spray in case of need (check specific ride rules regarding application of medications); halter; clean saddle pad and girth; and his spare shoes (just in case).

At rides it is most unusual not to find a friend, and even if you do not actually know anyone there, the endurance riding bunch are the friendliest people and there will always be someone willing to hold your horse while you make a trip to the john or get a drink. If you have a horse holder, do impress on him not to let the horse drink. I like to supervise this myself, and will go into it in more detail later in the chapter.

With all the gear placed ready to hand in the Landrover it is possible to manage without a helper. Even if I have one, I prefer to see to the horse myself, having the helper there for emergencies and additional help. However, on the really extended endurance rides of over 50 miles the picture changes, rider fatigue has to be taken into account, and the rider will need a breather at rest stops as well as the horse. Under these circumstances the helper becomes more important and he or she must be thoroughly briefed in all aspects of horse care during these layovers. When you ask a friend to act in this capacity make sure that he or she attends to the horse in exactly the same manner that you do; that way both you and the horse will be at ease. I always worry about placing the saddle and the pad beneath and girthing up, and always attend to that myself, even if I am lucky enough to have someone on hand for other chores. You may have other points you prefer to attend to yourself.

Give yourself plenty of time to check in at the start so there isn't a last minute rush. Once started, there is no need to charge forward, though many riders seem to disagree. I let the horse set out at a moderate trot for the first few hundred yards till he is in his stride and can move on more strongly.

After that I settle to pacing the horse according to the terrain.

You should have no worries about getting lost, since it is the routing officer's job to make sure his course is well marked, and this has been done very efficiently on all the United States rides in which I have taken part. Nevertheless it is essential to study the map in advance, particularly if you are not resident in the ride area, since this will give you a good idea of the terrain (shown by colors on the map) and gradients (shown by contour lines) over which you will be traveling.

Before all our really long rides, my friend Jane Nicholson and I lean very heavily on her husband, Douglas, who is first class at working out a time sheet to keep us on schedule. He makes up time cards showing two time checks: one at the required speed, and one a little above this speed. This way we know where we stand, and by referring to place names on the map and working out the times we should reach them, we know if we are slow, on time, or too fast. An added safeguard is that Douglas also meets us at given points on the map. By combining this with pacing our horses at speeds we have learned to recognize, we have a very good idea of just how many miles we have done, even in unknown countryside, and this double check means we don't have that sinking feeling of being way off schedule. Beware of helpful bystanders. A friend of mine competing for a Gold was once told, "You've plenty of time"; relying on this she reached the ride finish only to find she had missed Gold by three minutes.

On the very steep parts of the Golden Horsehoe ride at Cheltenham in Gloucestershire in 1973 we found we could not average more than 8 mph on the first half of day one, but picked up considerably on the last 25 miles, so that our overall average for the first 50 miles was 9.4 mph. The following day, using the same system, we averaged 9.25 mph but the ride was a little easier as there were not so many hills and it was simpler to even out our whole pacing. There was no point in traveling much faster than 9 mph, the extra ¼ mph just giving us an extra margin of time for a top award, providing we had full veterinary marks. Holding as even a pace as possible over the whole ride put less stress on the horses than if we had gone slowly in one section, only to have to really put on speed for

Nizzolan (*above*), American-bred Arabian stallion, exemplifies the good conformation of the first-rate endurance horse. He is clean-boned and well-fleshed but not overfleshed. His conformation makes for a smooth ride. In contrast, poor conformation in a horse (*below*) makes him unsuitable for endurance riding. His straight shoulders and pasterns prevent the desired long, fluid stride. Excess weight and bone produce a tiring ride.

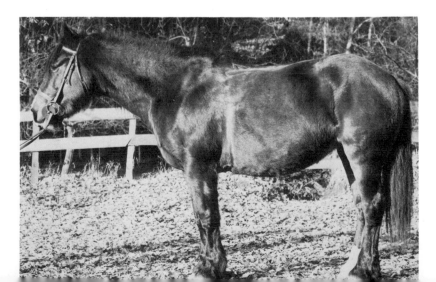

Poor conformation in motion: *Above*, note the lack of impulsion and reach in stride. *Below*, at the canter, the horse lacks drive. All the weight is on the forehand, putting excessive strain on shoulder and forelimbs and leaving the quarters relatively slack-muscled.

Above, Nizzolan is correctly run out for a soundness check. The loose rein permits natural action, and the handler's position allows the vet a clear view. *Below*, Nizzolan is incorrectly run out. The jerked rein raises his head, shortening the stride and preventing the vet from accurately judging soundness. The handler's position tends also to obscure the vet's view.

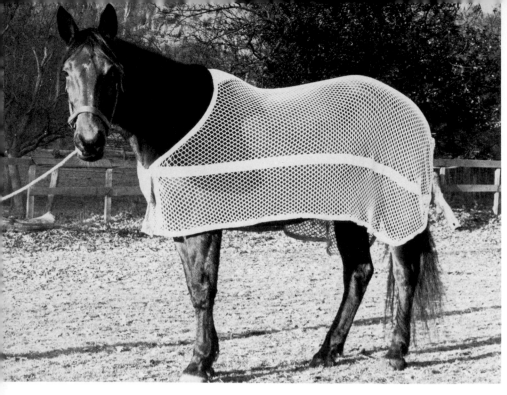

Magnet Regent demonstrates an incorrect cooler *above*. On a breezy day it will let chill air penetrate, thus lowering the body temperature too quickly. The lightweight cooler *below* is the best type to use. It permits the temperature to lower gradually and keeps the muscles warm.

The vet's examination: *Top left*, checking the sensitivity of the back; *top right*, checking the heartbeat; *bottom left*, checking the mucous membrane of the eye, salmon pink on a fit horse; *bottom right*, checking the leg for puffiness in tendons or ligaments.

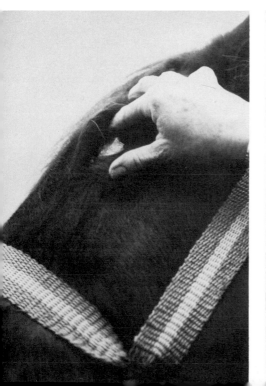 

Above, Nizzolan correctly tacked English style. (The saddle pad has been left off to show clearly the fit of the saddle.) Note the neat and trim-fitting bridle and the suppleness of the leather, which prevents chafing. *To the right*, correctly fitting saddle and pad show clear channel, permitting air through saddle gullet.

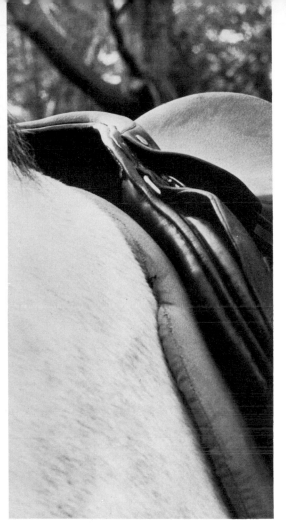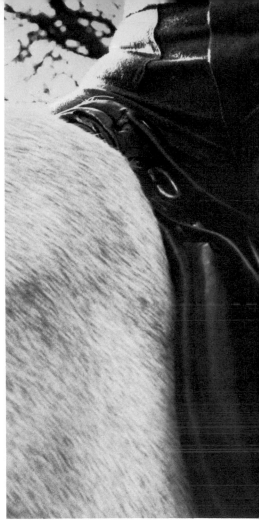

An ill-fitting saddle, the gullet press- ing on withers and spine. This can cause, at the very least, fistulous withers.

An incorrectly placed saddle pad, lying flush upon the withers. This can cause soreness and inflammation during a ride.

This two-page sequence shows five points in the course of Britain's Golden Horseshoe Ride, 1974—75 miles in two days. *Facing page, top,* Sandpiper Regency Gold, ridden by Brian Shepherd, and Nizzolan, ridden by the author, at the start. Note the keen forward-looking yet relaxed attitude of both stallions. *Middle,* Nizzolan on the right, approaching a high point after 4 miles of rough, steady climbing. Number 29 is the author's 14.2-hand paint pony Katchina. *Bottom,* coming up to the 50-mile mark at the end of the first day. Nizzolan's stride is still free though his flanks show some dehydration due to heat. *This page, top,* five miles from the finish, with plenty of zip in the stride despite lashing rain and strong winds, which plagued the second day—the last 25 miles—of the ride. *Bottom,* Nizzolan crosses the finish line with miles still in him. Note the pricked ears, free stride, relaxed head carriage. In this ride Nizzolan won a Golden Horseshoe and full veterinary marks.

Above, an unusual pair—the smallest in Britain's long-distance rides—Amanda Cox on her 12.2-hand pony Blue Peter. This tough and winning combination is proof that small ponies suitably mounted can ride with the big ones.

Right, Nizzolan, author up, climbing a New Forest hill on a 50-mile endurance ride.

Above, Wendell T. Robie of Auburn, California, has completed the Western States Tevis Cup 100 Miles One Day Ride fourteen times. Here he is shown on Nugget, Arabian gelding owned by John Rogers, nearing Squaw Peak (over 7000 feet above sea level), a few miles out from the starting point in Squaw Valley. Nugget later died in a barn fire.

Left, Lucille Kenyon and Pazzam, a winning combination on the East Coast circuit for many years. Pazzam was sired by the world-famous Arabian, Nizzam.

Donna Fitzgerald and Witezarif, four-time winners of the Tevis Cup. Here they are shown on their way to a win in the 100-mile Virginia City Ride in Nevada.

Matthew Mackay-Smith, D.V.M., on Sorya, his black Thoroughbred mare, at 8000 feet, Pleasant Valley, Colorado. Dr. Mackay-Smith is active both as a competitor and in veterinary control in the world of long-distance riding. He is a partner at the Delaware Equine Center, Cochranville, Pennsylvania.

long stretches later on. Even if you do not use maps, a time card geared to the 5-mile markers used in competitive trail riding is very handy.

During the ride I allow the horse as many drinks as possible from streams and clean puddles, but limit each to four to six swallows. This is beneficial because it helps a sweating horse to keep his fluid balance as near normal as possible, thus avoiding dehydration and cramping from too severe a loss. By drinking frequent small amounts he is in no danger of colicking, and at the halfway halt, rest stops, and evening halts he will not have such an overpowering craving for water. If you have a friend following you around the course and meeting you at intervals where the route crosses or comes near a road, the water problem is solved, but again watch the horse's intake.

If you really do have to go it alone and there is no water en route, be extra careful at compulsory halts. Allow the horse his six swallows, then pull him away, or, if you cannot manage this, tip the water out of his bucket. I know how very strong some horses can be when pulling for water. In about fifteen minutes he can have another six swallows, and in a 30-minute layover another six just prior to leaving for the second lap. On longer layovers it is safe to repeat the same small amounts, still limiting the intake but allowing a bit more over the whole period. Do not on any account let the horse swill a whole bucket. Small, well-spaced drinks will give him a chance to get the water back into his tissues. A larger quantity only sloshes around in his stomach and will inevitably cause colic if he is fatigued and then asked to proceed. At the earlier checks he will not be nearly as thirsty as he will be at later stops and back in stables after the day's stint is over.

Slow down for the last few minutes before arriving at compulsory veterinary and rest stops so the horse's heart rate will register a good reading and his respiration rate is subsiding. Also, if he reduces his output gradually, the sudden change from movement to standing to be checked and worked over is not as drastic as if he had bombed in the whole way. By all means bring him across the line looking as if he is ready for more. Visual impressions count for a lot.

Once through the vet check, start work on the horse. Most

rides have a 30-minute halt at halfway, longer endurance rides have hour-long checks spaced throughout the distance, and other rides, though not having an enforced halt, leave it to the wise rider to allocate enough time for necessary care in his route/time plan. Watering has already been covered. Give the horse a quick wipe over the face, around nostrils, mouth, and eyes, to refresh him. Get a cooler on immediately, but leave the saddle on. At some rides, the saddle has to be removed for vet check as soon as the horse comes in. In this case get it back on as quickly as possible, regirthing it a little more loosely. If you do not have to remove the saddle, leave it in place and, over the half-hour, loosen the girth gradually before taking the saddle off and replacing the wet saddle pad with a clean, dry one, as well as changing the dirty girth for a clean one. (But note: some United States rides do not permit *any* change of equipment unless something has broken.)

The reason for leaving the saddle on if possible (and no United States ride I have been on requires immediate saddle removal) is to prevent the blood from rushing into an area that has been under pressure, causing pressure bumps. Not all horses get these, but some definitely do. Pressure bumps nearly always mean the saddle is ill-fitting or too small for the rider's weight. The fit of the saddle may be incorrect only to a very minor degree; if it has not caused pressure bumps earlier, it is probably because the rider has not been in the saddle for as many consecutive hours in training as in the actual ride. (Discovering trouble at this stage does not mean necessarily that the saddle is totally unsatisfactory and should later be discarded; it may be only a matter of modifying the padding, for example.) If your horse does get pressure bumps on the ride, ice will help reduce them. If, however, you are on a ride whose rules forbid artificial aids and specify water at normal temperatures only, the bumps can be reduced, and the smallest one sometimes completely dispersed, by very gentle massaging from the center toward the edge. Be careful not to be too vigorous or you run the risk of pulling out hair and creating a problem that wasn't there to start with.

I find that at the brief stops there is little enough time to see to watering, cleaning up, checking for minor galls and hoof interferences, and changing wet gear, without taking the bridle off, putting the halter on, and then refitting the bridle. This is fine at the finish, but best left alone in minor checks as time can be more advantageously spent on other things as 30 minutes flash by. On stops which last for an hour the horse has more chance to unwind and nibble some hay, so do remove your bridle and let the horse relax. On no account should he be fed grain after traveling at speed over a fair distance. Many horses will get colic if you do this. The horse should not stand completely still for a whole hour's layover, particularly in the later checks. Much time will be taken up in veterinary examination and general care, and most of the balance should be granted as relaxation to the horse, but walk him for a few minutes once or twice so his muscles don't tie up. One of the things the vets will be watching for is whether the horse steps out willingly when he starts on the next section, and stiffening will prevent this. When resaddling, girth up carefully, making sure no skin gets pinched.

Ride the second and succeeding sections as carefully as the first, slowing down in the final mile so the horse has time to start pulse and respiration recovery before crossing the time line, and also so he conserves the energy to snap across that line looking great.

The real work starts after the ride, particularly on a three-day competitive trail ride or a really severe endurance ride, for it is back in the stables that the horse's true condition will show itself. He has been subjected to extreme stress; once movement has ceased he should relax, but he cannot do so if he is over-tired.

The horse will relax after a sensibly ridden ride but a stupidly ridden one, where excessive speeds have been asked from him, will ensure a bad recovery. In many cases, horses so ridden have colicked severely or had frighteningly bad heart rates; several have had heart attacks; some have never been the same horse again. This is not said to frighten people, but simply to warn them. In most cases where this happened the horse had not been properly conditioned nor the ride sensibly ridden.

We now come to the matter of care after the ride. I shall

describe the routine I follow on the Golden Horseshoe, where 50 miles are covered at speeds in excess of 9 mph on the first day to be followed by 25 on the second. Since similar care is needed by all horses under stress American riders can relate this to both endurance riding and competitive trail riding.

After a strenuous ride the horse will be extremely thirsty. He will have sweated considerable salt out of his system, and he will be tired. After the horse has been through his end-of-ride veterinary examination the first thing to do is to get his cooler on over the saddle, then unbridle him and put his halter on. Allow him a very few swallows of water, then walk him slowly so his muscles gradually unwind. If you put him away immediately he will stiffen and not be able to trot out freely the next morning for his veterinary check.

While he is walking I gradually loosen the girth over about a 30-minute period, slackening it a hole at a time. Since the pad underneath is saturated and clammy I slip it out without taking off the saddle once the girth is really slack and get a dry towel between saddle and horse. It sounds complicated, but in practice it isn't. At approximately 15-minute intervals I allow him a few more swallows of water, and after about half an hour he can be returned to his box to rest (if it is a chilly day, I would walk him a bit longer for cold air will tend to stiffen muscles rested too suddenly). Once in his box I leave his cooler on, allow him to nibble hay, but keep the water bucket out of his stable. Before letting him have free access to water I wait till he quits reaching for it; this generally takes about three hours. As he gets more water into his system I permit him a quarter of a bucket at a time. While he still wants water badly I put in a couple of ounces of salt (more for a large horse or if sweating has been excessive). He will be thirsty enough to drink it straight down and restore his salt balance. This is a better method than adding it to his feed which, since he is tired, he may or may not eat if he doesn't like the taste.

Once he has cooled down really well he can have the cooler taken off and then he will probably roll to scratch his hide. I do not bother cleaning the horse as soon as he is put in his stable. If he has a great deal of mud on him I remove the worst, but otherwise I let him alone to rest. Rest is the most important thing in the first hour after he goes into his box.

If it is a blistering hot day and air is still very warm, the horse can be sponged down after the ride with warm water (either sun-warmed if on a competitive trail ride or tap-warmed if there are no restrictions to water use). Cold water causes muscular contraction, just as in humans. The heat will have made him sweat much more profusely and he will feel better for a sponging and pick up quicker. Sponging takes less time than grooming so it can be done before he is left to himself. Also, if it is extremely hot and there is no breeze, he will not need the cooler, as it will act in reverse under those conditions.

At this point the horse's hard feed quota will be about 15 pounds a day and he will have had about a third on the morning of the ride split between normal and tiny feeds. That leaves 10 pounds of his daily ration. It would be very stupid to try to get all that into a tired horse. It is much better to cut his amount for one day than to overload his stomach and risk colic.

The timing of his feeding will need drastic alteration after a strenuous ride, so forget about normal evening feeding. About two hours after ride finish, I give a very small feed of about 1 pound and then over the remainder of the evening I aim to get more of the nine-pound balance into him split into three 2-pound feeds given at two-hourly intervals, the last around 11 o'clock. On this schedule his stomach is at no time overloaded and his digestion will not be strained. If he is too tired to eat, don't just pile one feed on top of another but see what he will clean up, and before going to bed leave about 2 pounds in his feed bucket for him to pick at. Unless you have declared the horse to be a fussy eater the fact that he leaves grain could lead the judges, who make a night round on competitive trail rides, to dock points as it is an indication of fatigue—a small point but worth knowing.

When he has eaten his first feed and is comfortably chewing on his hay, groom thoroughly, but don't take more time than is absolutely necessary. A tired horse is entitled to a touch of crankiness. Do the job and leave him alone, checking over the stable door periodically to see everything is all right.

If there is a hint of coolness in the night air, put a light blanket on him to stop his muscles tightening. It will pay off in extra suppleness the following morning. I make a final check about midnight, just looking in and not disturbing the horse. Between returning the horse to his box and that final check take him out two or three times, if permitted, for a very short walk to keep him limber.

Stable routine on the second morning will be basically the same as on the first, with the addition of a slightly longer period of limbering up, if permitted, prior to the morning vet check. If the horse is eager for his food all will probably be well. If he is not, but is sound and passed fit to resume the ride, watch out for signs of fatigue and coast him along rather than push him. The ride and stable routine for the 50-mile day should also be followed on the 25-mile day, and if the horse is excessively tired at the end of the 75, it may be wiser to postpone the journey home till the next day, particularly if he is not the best of travelers.

For American 100-mile-in-three-days rides there are rules concerning entering and leaving stables after ride finish. Once in his box a horse may not leave it till the nightly veterinary examination. Consequently I learned to take full advantage of the time allowed for cooling out, so that the horse's muscles had really unwound over a couple of hours where the pace was no more than an ambling walk. Ride rules also specify a morning opening and evening closing time for stables, so all care must be concluded within these time brackets.

An approximate day's schedule on a 100-miler, keeping the basics as for the Golden Horseshoe, but altering according to ride/time rules, would be:

Stables opening at 5 A.M. Feed around 4 pounds hard grain; muck out; put fresh water in bucket; adjust blanket; check for stiffness; then leave alone and get own breakfast.

7 A.M. Return and offer tiny 1-pound feed; groom thoroughly and encourage horse to shift around in his box.

7:30 A.M. Check self; tack up; girth lightly.

8 A.M. Ready for number to be called and start (most riders are away by 8:30 A.M. so adjust schedule accordingly).

With 40 miles to go in 6½ to 7 hours your time of arrival back at ride base will be around 2:45 P.M. Stables close between 8 and 9 P.M., times varying slightly with different rides, so you have 5¼ to 6¼ hours for all afterride care (this is assuming that you take advantage of the 30-minute timing leeway and use 15 minutes of it).

Use as much time as possible for cooling out. I used to leave two buckets of water to warm in the sun all day in front of the horse's box—one for the horse to drink and one for sponging off; then he was not subjected to sudden cold inside or outside.

With the horse back in his box by around 4:30 to 5 P.M. feeding can start. A 40-mile competitive trail ride stint is nowhere near as hard as 50 miles at 9 mph and over, so the feeding can quite happily be encompassed within the shorter time and, providing the horse is absolutely relaxed and not fatigued, more of his daily ration can be coaxed into him than after a hard-ridden endurance ride. If he is showing fatigue and/or stress, feed the same amounts as for the tougher rides.

After stables close the stable manager is there for an all-night watch so the rider can relax with a sense of security.

Feeding the Horse in Training

A good feeding program is a vital part of the management of the endurance horse, for without it he will not be able to produce the maximum effort needed to obtain top results. The horse must have the best feed available in the right quantity. It is no good trying to economize on grain and hay; if you do, the horse's condition will deteriorate and he will use up the reserves he needs for the all-out effort of a season of sustained work.

For competitive trail riding, if the horse is properly conditioned, has an equable temperament, and is an average feeder under all conditions, feeding levels can be kept constant, since there is only a minimal weight loss, if any at all other than that replaced within a day or two. However, at his peak output periods he cannot eat enough to actually replace the energy expended during, say, a two-day ride such as the Golden Horseshoe done at the higher speeds required for a Gold award, or the endurance ride of 50, 75, or 100 miles. Therefore he relies on his reserve to supplement the actual intake over the period of peak performance, and his temporary weight loss will be minimal, not enough to show visually but only on actual weighing or taping.

Careful feeding of the right rations in the proper quantities will enable the horse to withstand the strain. Poor quality feed, even if in greater quantity, will not give the nourishment required, so that the horse will continually work on his own reserves, having very little to sustain him in actual hard-ridden competition.

At the beginning of training the horse will be in relatively soft condition. Each owner will know which category his particular mount falls into: the easy keeper, the moderate, or the real hay and oat burner. Whatever his type the same, or basically the same, feeding methods should apply. A soft horse in light work will not burn up so much energy as the fitter animal in a further stage of training, so it follows that feeding will have to be geared to physical output. At first go easy on the grain, offering all the hay the horse wishes to eat.

A very broad guide to feeding, taking an average 1000-pound horse which with a medium build will stand around 15 hands, will be as follows:

(Rations shown are per 100 pounds of body weight.)

	GRAIN	HAY
Maintenance or light work up to one hour a day.	0.50 lb.	1.50 lbs.
Two hours' average work.	0.80 lb.	1.50 lbs.
Three to four hours' average work or two hours' hard work.	1.00 lb.	1.50 lbs.
Medium hard work up to six hours or three hours' hard work.	1.25 lbs.	1.25 lbs.
Latter stages of training when the pressure mounts.	1.50 lbs.	1.25 lbs.

This is only a very broad outline as each horse is, and should be treated as, an individual. This feed basis is for the horse that is a relatively easy keeper, but not the type that lives on the smell of feed, as some seem to do. I have two friends who both enter endurance and competitive trail rides in Britain. One, Mrs. Shuna Mardon, rides an Arab/Thoroughbred/Clydesdale cross 15.2-hand mare named Strathdon. This mare is of a very lively disposition, but her metabolic rate is very slow. In training she never eats more than 8 pounds hard feed a day, and consistently puts on weight. At the other end of the scale, Brian Shepherd's Palomino stallion, Sandpiper Regency Gold, a 15-hand Thoroughbred/Welsh Cob, eats upward of 24 pounds hard feed for the same energy output.

This horse has a very equable temperament. Nizzolan is a little above the average in his requirements, standing 15.1 and around 900–950 pounds weight, but he will eat around 9 pounds when idle, 12 when working normally, and 14 in hard work. When younger he ate more, so as he matures I expect he will be less expensive to keep. These are only three examples and given just so readers can see there is no rigid system for feeding, only a guide which sensible horsemen will adjust to their own animals.

With horses that have a higher metabolic rate the hard feed ration will need adjusting upward, and in that case I also allow them all the hay they will eat; unless they are absolutely compulsive eaters they will quit the haynet when they have had enough. With a compulsive eater, I do ration the hay as suggested above for medium keepers, fractionally more (about 16 pounds) for the horses with a higher metabolic rate, and correspondingly less for the really easy keepers. Many feed charts cut hay considerably for horses in hard work, but I have never found this to be necessary with any of the many different types I have conditioned for endurance work.

Not only amounts but types of feed are important to consider. For hay, a good timothy, or timothy and clover mix, is suitable. Alfalfa is also good. It is a very high-protein hay and if it is top quality, it can serve to cut the grain ration a little. It is difficult to buy in Britain but luckily I have a good source and I much prefer it, occasionally mixing it with some timothy. In the United States alfalfa is readily available and unless it gives your horse digestive upsets I would recommend using it. If it makes the droppings loose, mix it with another less rich hay as above. I have some horses who leave their grain in favor of alfalfa, and in Nizzolan's case he churns other hay into his bed, having gotten crafty about holding out for his favorite: he cleans up every wisp of alfalfa. Because the nutritional value is at its highest when grasses are in leaf, try to get first-cut hay, cropped before it goes to seed. Also avoid if possible hay that has been rained on; in the extended curing process it deteriorates in food value.

In the case of grains, again it is a matter of personal preference and individual horses whether you feed one exclusively or mix several types. The basic ration should be oats that are plump and clean and milky white when broken open, not poorly filled, more husk than grain. I prefer to use oats well crushed. When whole oats are fed, a certain proportion of them pass straight through the horse, wasting their food value. (This happens no matter how well the horse's teeth do their grinding job, but if it is excessive, his teeth need attention.) Whole oats do, however, have the advantage of not collecting dust. So don't buy too many crushed oats at a time.

If the horse is a little on the racy side or not particularly thrifty, I feed a certain amount of crushed barley, but not too much at one feeding because of overloading the stomach. In the United States corn can substitute for barley, as feeding values are approximately the same. Pelleted feeds can be used, but apart from the racehorse or high-protein variety which may be used as either an additional feed or complete short feed, I have not used them to any great extent. There are some brands specifically formulated for horses in hard work, and if it is impossible to get the top quality grain necessary I would rather use them because they do keep to a stated standard. However, I do not like using the type that enables you to dispense with hay as the horse becomes bored and will inevitably supplement his feed with part of his stable.

In addition to oats, a little barley (crushed or cooked and flaked) or flaked corn (not whole as it is extremely difficult to grind) and good quality bran are useful, although my own feeding system does not include much bran for a horse in hard work. I like adding molassine meal to feeds several times a week for palatability, variety, and the minerals it contains. Salt is one of the most important staples for a horse in hard training, and although regular feeds and hays contain a certain amount of natural salts the horse will sweat out more than these provide. Either mineral or plain salt can be used.

For the average horse that is receiving the 10-pound grain allowance a day, I would apportion his feed roughly as follows: oats, 6 pounds; barley, 2 pounds; high-protein nuts or pellets, 2 pounds. I add a pound of molassine meal to one feed every other day, and several times a week I add to the evening feed a couple of pounds of bran dampened with dissolved salt to make sure the horse is getting the salt he needs. (The other feed quantities are reduced accordingly.) If he will eat salt readily, keep a block in his manger or a salt holder in his stable; but I have found that some horses almost totally ignore their salt lick, while others nose it into their beds and crush it up, and it is too expensive to waste.

With the sweetfeed popular in the United States, care should be exercised over choice and amount fed. When I lived there I tried many varieties and various salesmen were always trying to proffer their companys' lines. In these I found that when price got competitive the feed quality sometimes suffered by the addition of too much molasses and nongrain fillers, causing horses to reject it. True, I always tried it out on the fussiest horse in the stable. The two I found best, not cheaper in price but cheaper because there was no waste, were Purina's Omolene and Eshelman's Red Rose, preferably the latter. Good sweetfeed can be super, as it contains a well-balanced selection of necessary feeds in addition to the obvious hard-grain ration. However, particularly when a horse is in very hard work and taking the maximum amount of hard feed, I prefer not to feed only sweetfeed but to substitute about 40 percent of the total weight with top quality crushed oats. In excessively hot weather watch for sweetfeed going sour if kept too long. Also, it should be kept in lidded containers as the molasses attracts flies.

Prior to his day off, give the horse a bran mash in place of his evening feed and add a bit of molassine meal and boiled linseed to it to make it tasty. Also, if you do have to cut back in his work for any reason, remember to also cut back in his grain intake. Azoturia is one of the hazards to watch out for in a horse that is suddenly rested, without grain reduction, after hard work.

The number of feeds per day varies according to the stage of training the horse is in and the total amount to be fed. (It can vary, too, for convenience, for with so many people fitting in their horse activities around a full-time job it is not always possible to stick to the preferred feeding schedule.) In early training when the horse is not getting much grain I feed morning and evening, giving him all his hay at night as he is out in the day. Later on, as feed increases, he gets a midday feed, again haying only at night. In the last stages, when he really gets a tremendous amount of grain, I feed four times, the last feed just before I go to bed. The midday feed is always the smallest.

One point to remember—and one that is not generally thought about—is that although a feed or grain may be described as containing, for instance, "13 percent protein" that is not the total digestible nutrient value. The nutrient value is only about half that percentage or a little over, so you can see why it is important to give the horse only the best hay and grain, as during extremely hard work he will need the protein to repair body tissues and the carbohydrates to produce the energy. If you cannot get the quality feeds you would like—and these days it is becoming more difficult to do so, particularly in the case of hay, which can be real rubbish—be advised by your vet as to which supplement or additive to use with the feed. The feed company representative, although selling a good product, may not have the one best suited to your own horse's requirements.

A further word about quality of feed, both hay and grain. Land constantly used for producing one type of crop will eventually be depleted in certain respects. It is therefore a good plan, unless you purchase commercial feedstuffs with minerals, salts, and vitamins and trace elements added, to be fussy about your source. Some growers do not rotate their crops, but use the same fields year in year out for them. If feasible, soil analysis will enable you to be sure of getting grains and hays containing the right food elements in the right quantities. If you use poor quality feed grown on depleted soil, the horse's condition will suffer, and he will not thrive as he should. He may appear first-rate but under stress he will not come up to scratch because of a dietary deficiency.

Tack

NO matter what equipment you use in any riding activity it should always be correctly fitted to the horse, kept in good repair, and clean, particularly the parts in contact with the horse's hide. This is especially important with the endurance horse as he wears tack for very long periods at a time and is extremely active while wearing it.

Saddles

The constant powerful movement of muscles over the back area for long periods of time means that the endurance horse requires a supremely well-fitting saddle. It should be contoured to the horse's back so that as perfect a fit as possible is achieved. Great attention should be paid to the stuffing as well as to the structure of the saddle.

When you are choosing the ideal English saddle, several points must be considered. The prime one, of course, is fit. Apart from the saddle being contoured to the horse's back, the front arch should be clear of the top of the withers by a minimum of two fingers' and a maximum of three and a half fingers' depth, that is, with the weight of the rider in the saddle. If a saddle is too wide in the gullet, it will drop down and the spine will bear the pressure that should be carried by the bars of the saddle. If it is too narrow, the saddle will sit too high, affect the rider's position, and result in the side of the withers and the top of the shoulders being pinched and bruised.

In addition to correct basic structure, the stuffing should be properly proportioned. Too much stuffing in the rear of the sad-

110/

dle will tip the rider forward, and although weight should be carried over the shoulder section and forehand, too disproportionate a weight there could dig in over the shoulders, causing lack of proper shoulder movement which could hinder and cause distress to the front legs, resulting in strains. It may also result in pressure on the withers, causing heat, soreness, friction, etc. Too much stuffing in the front section will send the rider back onto the cantle, thus putting undue weight on the kidney and loin area—a vulnerable part of the horse's anatomy—which will also affect his propulsion.

An incorrectly stuffed saddle could result in saddle movement, which will gall a horse. Slightly incorrect stuffing is not always at first apparent, as I once learned to my cost; a saddle I was using appeared a perfect fit when I rode in flat country, but on hills the front arch rocked, causing minor chafing over my horse's lower wither and shoulder region.

During the horse's progressive training period when he will go from soft to moderate to really hard condition, his wither, shoulder, and back areas will show a marked change of shape (as will the rest of him, but that is not the subject of this chapter). The withers will become more prominent as fat fines down. Shoulders will reduce in fat and build up in muscle; over the back, too, the fat will disappear and muscles will become strong and elastic, showing considerable movement under the skin. Therefore the saddle that fits at the outset of training may well need a stuffing adjustment during the training period. For this it is useless just to take the saddle to the saddler and request a restuffing or additional stuffing. You must examine the whole saddle, not just the points that you know need attention, by trying it out on the horse. Then make a careful record to present to the saddler with the saddle. It is worth paying a little extra to have the saddler come out to see the horse or to take the horse to the saddler if either is at all possible. If, as is quite likely, it is not, you will need to take very special care in purchasing your saddle to begin with and in instructing the saddler on later adjustments.

Buying the cheapest variety of either the English or Western style is no economy, for it could prove infinitely more expensive than a really good higher-priced saddle if the horse's back suffers and he is laid up in training or penalized in competition for galls, etc. In the cheaper sorts there obviously have to be economies made to bring the price down.

The areas which are most likely to suffer in the English variety are in the tree, which may have a tendency to spread, and in the panels under the flap, which may just have a leather-covered tree, then the skirt over it. Without the full-panel lining there could be pressure from the lower edge of the tree in the upper shoulder region. Also, the whole saddle is likely to deteriorate with stress; the leather will not be so good; in some cases the contouring will be at fault, putting the rider in one of the poor positions previously mentioned which in turn bring their own problems.

With the Western saddle, although the basic shape is the same as for better quality saddles, again the contouring may sit the rider in the wrong position. Also, the tree will in all likelihood be only sparsely covered and have many pressure points, and the structure of the tree will naturally be cheaper and more likely to split, especially if made of wood.

Once the tree on either an English or a Western saddle has spread or split, damage can be done to the horse's back, so in choosing a saddle take extra care and look at several; if possible, get them on approval (you don't buy shoes without trying them on). However, if in doubt, do try to get the services of a saddler. He will not only advise for immediate purchase but give tips on what to look for in the future as training alters the horse's shape. It will definitely pay dividends in the long run. If you can't do this, pay careful attention to the *exact* conformation of your horse; the careful choosing of a saddle should result in comfort for both horse and rider. The Western saddle of good quality seems to present fewer fitting problems than the English variety, mainly I think because the latter is so exactly contoured to the horse's back that any discrepancy can cause problems, but on a long ride for comfort I prefer the English saddle; the extra width and rigidity of a Western saddle are tiring. Also I can feel the horse's back muscles and movement that much better through an English saddle, but this is just personal preference.

When asking for a saddle to be restuffed, stipulate you want exactly that, not just packing in additional stuffing on top of the old. This often results in the old stuffing's being packed and jammed in so hard and lumpily that it starts up pressure lumps on the horse's back. A soft, even-textured material should be used; layered lambswool is recommended by my saddler, not the mess of carpet fillings he took out of one almost new saddle I took in for attention. No saddle should be stuffed to maximum capacity, as that prevents correct contouring to the horse's back. After a week or so of use the stuffing settles and the saddle should be returned if necessary for further attention. The same applies with a new saddle and is usually a service included in the initial cost.

Not only should the saddle fit the horse, but it should be comfortable for the rider, and as far as possible aid in maintaining the correct position on the horse's back. For this position a knee and thigh roll is advantageous, but do not confuse this with the extra forward seat of the showjumper. The best is a deep-seated, general-purpose saddle which will relieve pressure on the kidneys. When this is used with a long stirrup, contact with the horse will be maintained.

Another aspect of saddle choice is whether to have a spring or rigid tree, and this is largely a matter of personal choice. My own preference is for the rigid tree. It is stronger, and the bars have a wider bearing surface, thus spreading the load better. The thinner width of the spring tree bars are subject to both normal stresses of a saddle and metal fatigue, which will result in a fissure, most often in the front arch, necessitating costly repairs.

Ideally a saddle should be used on only one horse, but these days with the general high cost of saddlery this is not often possible, particularly if the horse's shape changes considerably during training. But do avoid using the same saddle on backs with widely differing characteristics, as somewhere along the line a tree will be spread and no longer fit the horse it was first intended for.

Saddle Pads

These days very few riders ride without using saddle pads. These should not be used merely to alleviate pressures of an ill-fitting saddle. Unless padding is very thick this will not be achieved, and if excessively thick padding is used, it may have the undesirable effect of forcing the bars apart and thus lowering the saddle onto the horse's spine, so that the bars cannot do the job they were designed for.

There are many types of pads on the market. The best is a very dense, cushioned double-pile acrylic fiber. It is expensive but worth it as it is highly absorbent, does not draw the back, remains in place, and does not wrinkle or pinch. The next best and less expensive is the shaped pad with a fairly dense foam pad interleaved between two layers of thick cotton twill. The twill absorbs sweat and dirt while the foam cushions and spreads pressure over larger areas.

Acrylic single-fiber pads are too thin to be of any real use as padding. A linen "tea towel" variety is bad on an endurance ride as it often wrinkles and consequently pinches. Its only real use is to keep the saddle clear of the dirt and sweat that work and heat build up.

Sheepskin is very absorbent and provides a fair cushioning, but it has two disadvantages. It is difficult to keep clean, since washing hardens the skin; and constant use tends to mat the wool into a lumpy texture.

Felt padding is good providing it is not too thick; ¾ inch is the maximum. It is highly absorbent and does not draw the back, but it is difficult to keep really clean and cannot be washed as easily as other types.

Nylon, while looking neat and being very easily washable, slips and definitely draws the back, allowing no absorption of sweat at all. Because it slips, the nylon pad invariably drags down over the withers, causing pressure.

One of the best pads is natural wool folded into several thicknesses as it is highly absorbent and, being a natural fiber, does not draw. Thick uncovered foam padding is to be avoided because it does not successfully absorb dirt and sweat and, particularly if it is too thick, it permits the saddle to roll somewhat.

The Western saddle padding which consists of a felt and hair pad and a wool blanket can also be used under an English saddle, and in terms of sweat absorption, nonslip, and no drawing attributes, it is very good. The only thing to watch with this is that it is not too thick for the saddle you are using.

All padding should be kept scrupulously clean, as the back

area is one where many penalty points occur in long-distance riding.

All padding, whether used on a Western or English saddle, should be pulled up into the arch or gullet of the saddle so it does not drag across the withers, causing pressure. Natural fibers will tend to grip the horse and stay where you put them, whereas nonnatural ones such as nylon and silky rayon blankets will slide down between saddle and horse. Thick dense-fibered acrylic does not do this. I find the best fixing methods with English pads are the velcro fastenings, as they stay put. Elastic does not, and neither are the billet (girth) tapes very good for positioning.

Western Saddles and Pads

Many riders prefer the Western or Stock saddle, and most of the above comments about fitting a saddle to the horse apply to both the Western and English varieties. The type of saddle preferred is up to the individual, but the tree of the Western saddle again falls into three basic types—wide, narrow, or medium gulleted. The bars are of a different shape—more of the back is actually under pressure and consequently the weight-carrying surface is spread over a wider area, which is definitely to the good.

All Western saddles should be used with blankets and pads. A thin blanket is insufficient, as it will twist and slip. The ideal is a thick hair or hair and felt mixture pad first, then a folded wool blanket. Some thick wool or Navajo weave blankets are thick enough to dispense with the felt pad.

Points to watch for in a Western saddle are that the sheepskin lining to the saddle doesn't become worn. The saddle strings are fixed through leather conchos into the saddle tree and these, though usually covered by a thin layer of acrylic or sheepskin fiber, can cause pressure points on the horse's back. Also, some horses tend to rub behind the cantle where the saddle pad moves slightly, usually when the saddle doesn't fit perfectly and moves slightly across the loin area.

The advantage of a Western saddle is that weight is better spread over the horse's back and pressure points are less likely to occur. The disadvantages are the greater weight, and the fact that there is no air channel since the rear housing of the saddle is flush with the horse's back. With a horse prone to pressure problems I would rather take a bit of extra heat buildup under the saddle than chance pressure bumps arising if I knew switching from English to Western could avert them.

Girths

With English saddles there are many varieties of girth but they fall into two main categories: leather and the nylon and cotton fiber string variety. I have found that with some horses used for endurance work the hair tends to rub if a leather girth is used, even if it is kept clean and supple. I much prefer the cotton string variety. These grip well, absorb sweat so no chafing occurs, and are easy to wash—at the end of a ride I just rinse them well and leave them to dry, soaking them occasionally overnight in hot suds. Also they are cheaper, three string ones being approximately equivalent to one leather one in price. If you do prefer leather, use Balding, Lonsdale, or Beaufort, which are contoured so that no chafe occurs around the elbow area.

Western girths or cinches are all of the string variety but differ in width quite a bit, from medium wide to very wide. Note should be taken of the horse's girth area to see if a wide or medium wide cinch is best. Usually the medium width one is best because the excessively wide girths can extend too far forward and come into too close proximity to the elbow and the tender skin just behind it. Some Western girth rings also tend to chafe the hair. If this is the case, a sheepskin-backed leather guard can be purchased that will help prevent this.

Bridles

Bridles used on endurance horses should be as simple as possible with a bit that is comfortable and preferably of fairly thick construction; thin bits can cut, cause abrasions, deaden nerves, and cause tensions which will reflect on the horse's performance. If fitted too loosely, the leather parts can chafe, and the bit may be incorrectly placed in the horse's mouth. Conversely, if fitted too tightly, it can cause restrictions.

An endurance horse will travel differently because collection, as basically understood, will be absent. Instead, he will be more inclined to reach with head and neck, and there will be great distension of nostrils and windpipe. Therefore particular attention should be paid to noseband and throatlatch so that no constriction is present. This does not apply to the horse needing corrective bits or nosebands, such as drop or grackle, and with these the rider will have to arrive at the solution whereby the horse is under control but unhampered in performance.

Martingales

Although martingales are used mainly as corrective measures for a horse with poor head carriage, I find them handy on a horse that sometimes raises his head in resistance against control. A running martingale prevents this with no fretting on the horse's part. A horse with his head carried too high is far more trip-prone through imbalance than one with a good low natural head carriage, on whom the martingale only acts to counter resistance. The horse soon learns how to relieve himself of the martingale's pressure and thinks twice about resisting.

Breastcollars

Breastcollars are very useful pieces of equipment which nearly all endurance horses will need at some time in their competitive careers. They prevent saddles from slipping back on sharp inclines, as even the best-fitting saddle will do if the going is steep enough. There are several types to choose from and, with English equipment, the best is the hunting breastcollar which is shaped to the horse, thus preventing breath restriction. It also holds its place better. Choose one in fairly wide leather as, within reason, the broader the leather the more area there is to spread pressure over. Too narrow a leather strip will chafe over a sustained period. A rounded shoulder section is also good as there are no edges to cut or press into skin, but these are considerably more expensive to have made.

With Western breastcollars, the best are those which have a slight "V" at the chest, being contoured to the horse's shape. They should be in wide leather; if the horse's shape is such that the saddle goes back without the aid of a breastcollar in normal work, the extra hillwork will put added pressure on the chest area, so a sheepskin lining is advisable to soften and lessen pressures. The contoured shape prevents pressure on the horse's windpipe. Any pressure there, as could be the case if the breast-collar were attached too high, could both restrict his breathing rhythm and raise his head carriage, which could in turn affect his way of travel. The most natural way is to be encouraged as that means economy of stride and economy of energy expended. Mohair and/or natural fiber breastcollars are also very good, especially if the horse is thin-skinned; leather, no matter how supple, chafes.

Brushing Boots

There are many types of brushing boots. Some ride rules do not permit them. Some do. Actually, a horse that brushes badly enough to really damage himself is not ideal for the type of work entailed. Slight brushing can often be overcome by the farrier, or by muscling up as condition improves. Wearing brushing boots often invites the additional hazard of mud and small pieces of grit working between boot and hide, causing friction and resulting in penalties and soreness for the horse. However, if it is decided to use brushing boots, do not use felt. Almost certainly there will be water to cross enroute; also there may be snaggly briars alongside or trailing in the pathways to be ridden; felt will be adversely affected by both.

Much the same comments apply to the horse needing over-reach boots as to those needing brushing boots.

Once you have the correct tack keep it clean, supple, and checked for wear. Bits should be looked at occasionally to make sure no joints are wearing thin and no movable pieces which come into contact with the horse are burring against each other, causing sharp edges that can cut. If this happens, file smooth or, if excessively worn, exchange for a new bit.

Running a Ride

WITH long-distance rides becoming more popular and part of many riders' yearly fixture lists it is more than likely that a regular competitor may find himself called upon to organize a ride, since the most obvious choice for organizer is someone who is dedicated to the sport. In this case it may be helpful to be able to draw on someone else's experiences.

Over the past few years I have been involved in running several British Horse Society qualifying rides for the Golden Horseshoe Endurance Ride and also both competitive and pleasure rides for the Endurance Horse and Pony Society. The more recent rides have definitely gone better than the earlier ones, as mistakes and omissions have been corrected in succeeding years.

Basically all long-distance rides need the same framework of organization, with the less-complicated pleasure rides being the easiest to run, and competitive events demanding a lot more attention to detail.

When you have decided to run a ride your first move should be to gather your key officials and working committee together and list the many points which will have to be covered. Briefly they are:

1. The ride venue and the facilities available.
2. The ride rules and awards for successful competitors.
3. Judges and veterinarians, farriers, doctors, etc.

4. The route and its marking.
5. Budget.
6. Catering.
7. Advertising and reportage via press.
8. The ride day.
9. Afterride tidying up, etc.

Any ride's success depends on three main factors: (1) *The competitors.* They should be assured they will have a well-planned and well-marked route to ride over; that the judges will be competent in the field of long distance and/or endurance riding; that the facilities provided will be adequate. Nothing deters competitors more from future participation than discovering lacks in any of these elements; (2) *smooth organization;* (3) *good base facilities.* These are particularly important for the judges and officials, as a successful ride is one that can be assured of a repeat running and word soon gets around if facilities are bad or nonexistent. Not only will the same judges and helpers not give their services again, but it will be very difficult to find replacements.

Prior organization is vital to the success of a ride. You must allow plenty of time for organization and leave nothing to chance. Pleasure rides tend to be more localized regarding entry, have a shorter route, and need correspondingly fewer officials than endurance or competitive trail rides, so though organization must be good the scope is narrowed, and a shorter time for preparation is all right. However, if it is to be an annual event run on competitive lines it is important to have an initial meeting at least six months prior to the event. All the following notes are written on the assumption you are working on a competitive ride, and organizers can select the relevant details for running other rides.

The first year's ride will be the most difficult to run and much will be learned that will help in subsequent years.

At the outset draw your committee together. Keep it small and composed of people who are really prepared to work, not just full of promises to see things done and/or advice as to what needs doing without actually taking on their fair share of the burden.

Draw up a list of key positions for the ride, the main ones being:

1. Secretary.
2. Course Setter.
3. Chief Ride Steward.
4. Announcer.
5. Timekeeper.
6. Ride Marshal.
7. Ride Hostess.
8. Judges' and Vet's Recorders.
9. Runners.

The Secretary is responsible for the overall running of a ride. In committee, main tasks will be discussed and jobs shared among members. The Secretary should see that each person knows what is wanted. After that members should liaise with the Secretary, but should not need constant reminders, as this only makes a difficult job doubly hard. The Secretary will be responsible for any correspondence about entry forms, for contacting judges, for arranging for police assistance and first aid, for dealing with the owner of the ride base, and for ordering ribbons and other awards. All financial details will go through him, such as paying for veterinarians' services, awards, and the expenses incurred by various ride officials.

The Course Setter should be a person with an eye for country; should know the particular route with all its hazards exceptionally well; and should be able to get along with any landowners through whose property the ride is to be run. (The personal approach is best here, backed up by a letter from the Secretary.)

The Chief Ride Steward will be responsible for choosing the stewards, both mounted and dismounted, and positioning them around the course. It is most important that stewards realize they are there for competitors' guidance, and that they should not bunch up and gossip or drift off before the last numbered competitor has passed them. The Chief Steward should make sure that each steward is provided with a complete list of competitors and their numbers, with all the horses which have been scratched deleted from the list as far as possible. (There will always be a few entries who just do not turn up on the day, but that is one of the things organizers cannot guard against.) The Chief Steward and Course Setter should work closely together.

The Announcer, Timekeeper, and Ride Marshal should work very closely together, and additional runners should be assigned to each so that liaising is efficient on the day.

The Announcer will be responsible for calling competitors to the start, and the *Timekeeper* will note their departure and arrival times, plus any penalties in time over the course, as well as the allowances for any holdups, should these be permitted. The Timekeeper's job is most important, as some horses run very close to permitted time and in rides where time penalties are given it could mean the difference between winning, placing, or simply completing a ride. *The Ride Marshall's* job is to oversee the smooth function of the ride base on the day of the event. He is also responsible for liaising between competitors and officials.

The Ride Hostess has an important and very thankless task, as often her job can make or mar the day for the judges, veterinarians, and outside helpers. She is responsible for catering; if a club wishes to keep everybody happy, it is essential to provide good food, with hot drinks on a cold day and the opposite for hot weather. It is a considerate touch if soap, nail brushes, basins, towels, and hot water can be provided for the vets and judges. If base facilities provide these very close to the judging area that is fine, but if not, such things should be readily available and set out in a cleared trailer, a caravan, or, failing that, in the back of a pickup truck.

Judges' and Vets' Recorders. Each judge and/or vet should have an assistant assigned to him for the whole day whose job is to write down any particulars on each horse's score sheet.

Runners. It is always useful to have several extra people available for the many additional jobs that crop up at the last minute and that no amount of good organization can completely foresee.

Ride Venue

The choice of venue is most important. Ideally a base

should be selected from which the course can be laid through testing riding country. If the riding country is not ideal, but the proposed base has good facilities, it would be wise to give it serious consideration; the ride's success depends upon several factors, not least of which is keeping all the officials happy. Your own club or society members may be willing to put up with discomfort, but visiting judges, vets, etc., should be treated with care and consideration.

It is no good having a ride base situated out in the wilds— even though the surrounding area is the best riding imaginable —if it is inaccessible or lacks communications either on the grounds, or very close by in case a rider or horse gets injured and an ambulance or trailer is needed in a hurry. Neither should it be completely open to the weather with no shelter available for officials who do not have the benefit of keeping moving.

The facilities should include an area large enough to park trailers so they do not interfere with the running of the ride. There should be an ample grassy area for walking horses prior to and after the ride. An area must be kept entirely for judging and veterinary examinations; it must include a level, hard surface for trotting horses out for soundness. Stony ground is bad as a horse may inadvertently hit a sharp stone, jeopardizing his chances. A slope is also bad, as a fair soundness runup must be done on level ground. Grass is no good, as some horses appear sound on soft going but are shown unsound when trotted on a hard surface. Also in a very few cases unsoundnesses are barely detectable and the ears must come to the help of the eyes, which is impossible except on smooth, hard going.

There should be watering facilities for horses and some form of catering for competitors. Clean toilet arrangements are a must. Ideally there should be a telephone either at the site, or extremely handy. Electricity, to which the PA system can be hooked, is an advantage, as megaphones are often less than satisfactory.

Ride Rules and Awards

These should be drawn up well in advance, clearly stated in entry forms, and adhered to strictly. All relevant ride details should also be clearly stated. Awards should, at the very minimum, allow for one rosette or certificate to each successful competitor. If a winner and places are also to be awarded, these should be in addition to completion awards. Organizers will attract a higher entry if a "Best of Various Categories" rosette is also awarded, and the known local competitive and potential competitive field will give a very good idea as to what would best suit specific areas.

Order rosettes, certificates, trophies, etc., well in advance. I think it better, though an added expense as the leftover rosettes cannot be used later on, to specify place and date on the awards, not just club name and ride.

Judges, Veterinarians, Farriers, and Doctors

Immediately after settling the rules and dates of entry, contact the judges, veterinarians, farriers, doctors, and any other outside assistants needed.

The judges and veterinarians are the most important. Nearly all rides are judged by vets, though some have vets plus a "lay" judge who is a known horseman competent in this field of judging. Approach the vets a good six months prior to the event, giving them exact details of what will be required of them, and expect to pay a realistic fee, plus expenses, for their work. Although much of their free time is given voluntarily to various shows, they are too often exploited to a greater or lesser degree. If they feel a society or club is doing its best not to impose on them, they will be more inclined to help.

Do not ask two vets from the same practice. Even if they should agree, it is very possible one will be called away on an emergency. Also, if possible, try to get one more vet than is minimally necessary in case one of the others cannot work on the day or you are confronted with one of those unfortunate situations when a vet is called away to an accident, leaving the judges at base shorthanded. Judges should not be asked to cope with more horses than feasible, and the way the ride is to be run and the depth of each veterinary examination will dictate how much vets and judges can be expected to handle with the efficiency and thoroughness required.

Farriers also have a pretty tight working schedule and Saturdays, when most rides are held, are often fully booked either by people who work weekdays and have shoeing appointments over the weekend, or by the farrier's being on call at some show. So engage a farrier's services early.

There should be a doctor, a qualified nurse, or a first-aid person present throughout the ride and, here again, early notification is best.

The police should be informed well in advance if you wish their cooperation. It is always good policy to advise them of any competition going on which will entail a number of horses either traveling alongside or crossing any busy roads. I have found the police very helpful in providing officers to assist at dangerous crossings. In one case when a horse had badly staked itself, it was due to the police officer's prompt use of his radio that the vet and horse transport arrived in minutes, and the officer assisted the vet in the care of the injured horse.

The Route and Its Marking

The route should be planned via the Geodetic Survey map and then ridden. Consult local riders for advice. Remember when the route is first planned, which will probably be in winter, that ground conditions will alter seasonally. When working out the ride length and route on the map, remember that contours should be taken into account and that in very hilly country an approximate fifth of the distance shown as hilly on the map will have to be added to your distance count to allow for rise and fall in the actual route. It could be disastrous on a ride where the achievement of a place depends on good timing if competitors found the actual route was longer than that advertised in the schedule. Therefore, check the entire distance with a surveyor's measuring wheel.

When riding the route note good sections where competitors can make time, and bad parts where speed will be impaired. Also note such hazards as holes, bogs, gravel, gates, and roads —anything, in fact, that could slow a competitor—detailing their surface, type, etc. Too many time-consuming hazards are unfair, as competitors have a right to be able to keep to a reasonable average, and if a ride schedule states the required speed it must be possible for the average horse to do this without extreme difficulty. Rules and time allowance should be to the fore when you are planning the route.

Ensure that enough time has been allowed to complete the ride without the competitors' being forced to cover any section of the course at excessive speed. The course should not be so easy that no challenge is offered but it is better to provide that challenge through stiffer terrain than through hazards. The Course Setter will need plenty of help in laying out the route as this is one of the vital points upon which success depends. He will also need to coordinate closely with the Chief Ride Steward as to the placing of stewards along the course.

The type of country crossed should offer plenty of variety to be a real test of endurance, but it should avoid roadwork as much as possible. It is necessary to obtain permission to ride across private land. Note danger crossings on roads so that police can be advised and asked for help.

Route marking is a very time-consuming job, and generally the whole thing has to be done only a day or two prior to the event itself, particularly when the route lies across open country needing no permission to ride over. In the New Forest where I live, one of the main ride hazards is that, however late the markers are put out, "persons unknown" with a warped sense of humor delight in removing them, thus making it very difficult to be sure of the trickier turns en route. Here we have found the best answer, apart from late marking and the presence of stewards, is for a local competitor, usually one of those on the ride committee, to go first, so that some warning of this hazard is reported to the closest steward. We had a complete mile of markers removed one year, but owing to rapid repairs by the Chief Ride Steward the chaos that could have resulted was averted in time.

Another tip for facilitating route following is for all local competitors who know the route to wear colored armbands, so that nonlocal competitors, should they get lost or be unsure of the way, can team up with, or get route advice from, one of these riders. When marking, make sure marker posts are bedded firmly in the soil. Carry appropriate tools in the pickup truck when course setting.

All details of route marking should be stated clearly in the ride schedule; over the years two methods have proved the most satisfactory. These are:

1. *The three-color system* using: red posts for a right turn, white posts for a left turn, blue posts for straight on.
2. *The one-color system* with turns indicated by an additional post or disk very close to the corner marker to indicate the path to take.

Five-mile markers are highly appreciated by competitors; unless riders are well versed in map reading and have a photographic memory, they find markers more useful than maps for guidance in pace rating. Novice endurance riders, in particular, may not have a very clear idea of rating without mileage reminders every so often.

It should be remembered by the organizers that the ride is a test of the horse's endurance, not the rider's map-reading ability! Although some riders find a written description of the course a useful supplement to a map, it will not be of much use to strangers to the area who will not recognize "Farmer Smith's hayfield" or "Farmer Jones's duckpond." Riders cannot be expected to constantly stop their horses and pull out ride descriptions and maps to study their location, especially on a wet and windy day or on a spooky horse.

The markers themselves should be painted in a strong color which shows up well from a distance. Fluorescent orange is ideal for this. Markers can be made from a variety of materials; the most usual are:

1. Stakes about four to six feet high.
2. Large disks about a foot in diameter and painted on both sides.
3. Large, brightly colored plastic bags (usually blue fertilizer bags).
4. Surveyor's tape.

Whatever markers are used there should be plenty of them and they should be securely fixed. In dimly lit woods stakes may not show effectively and surveyor's tape or large strong tags suspended from trees and bushes are good. Where the path winds or is not very clear the markers should be spaced so that the next one is visible from the one being passed.

Practically the entire course should be accessible by a pickup truck or Jeep to facilitate course setting; markers for the very few stretches that cannot be reached that way can be set out from horseback. Bear in mind that an injured horse may have to be picked up en route, so route accessibility at close intervals is a must. When fixing above-ground markers, bear in mind that eye level to a person on horseback will be much higher up than to a person on foot, so place markers appropriately.

Types of route marking that have failed are arrows that can be reversed or slue around in the wind, and disks or other small devices that tend to be hidden by foliage and bypassed because of their size. The main thing to remember is to use plenty of strikingly colored and well-fixed markers, whatever their design.

Budget

All ride income is from entry fees, which should be decided on at the first committee meeting. The entry fee should be a realistic figure. Riders get real value for money in these events, which include a veterinary examination, a whole day's riding, and good company in which to ride, whereas at a show they are in the ring a scant thirty minutes or so or, if jumping, their performance is reckoned in seconds.

The schedule should state if fees are refundable. If they are not, it is easier to work out a budget. If they are, bank on a 15 to 20 percent withdrawal. Even if the rules state that there will be no refunds, the committee should be prepared to make exceptions in certain cases, such as horse or rider illness, but only on production of a doctor's or veterinarian's signed certificate and then only if received before the entry closing date.

Decide on the maximum number of entries you will accept. Research into your prospective entrants should give you an idea of what your entry will be, as most rides start by interested people saying, "What a good idea, so and so would like to enter."

Entry number depends on the locality. If the ride is across

good open country, the entry will be correspondingly high, and a large number of your entires will be from people not blessed with good riding in their own locality. However, at least 60 percent of entries are normally from home territory, although this is not always the case.

The breakdown of likely entrants, apart from the "dedicated core" of endurance riders, would be:

1. Those who ride for pleasure. They are usually very keen, particularly if they like competitive events but do not enter shows.
2. Youngsters. They usually show a lively interest, as it is another area in which to learn about horsemanship.
3. Riding club members. They usually account for a fair percentage of entries.

Showing people are, on the whole, not interested. Their animals, if put into ride condition, would not be in the accepted show condition. Hunting people, at present, can see no point in endurance riding, with the exception of those who hunt to ride, enjoying the equine more than the canine side of the sport.

Having decided on the possible prospective entry, the breakdown of expenses will be approximately as follows:

1. The heaviest part, taking at least 50 percent of the total, will be the judges' and/or vets' fees, plus those of the farrier. Get these to state in advance how much their fees will be, and keep an additional sum in mind to cover their expenses.
2. Awards will be up to 15 percent of the total.
3. Catering will be about 10 percent.
   Out of the remaining 25 percent organizers will have to get:
4. Postage.
5. Telephone.
6. Gasoline for course setting and various trips occasioned by the ride, plus incidentals such as marker paint, stationery, advertising, and printing costs.

All rides are run on a lot of goodwill and free service and time is rarely costed at full value. Vets usually charge a minimal fee, and organizers are lucky to get the tip of the iceberg of such costs as gasoline, postage, and telephone bills.

A first event does well to break even, as such reusable items as markers and numbers have to be purchased, so expect a small loss to be taken out of funds on a first attempt. In later years the Secretary will know how to make a few economies.

Pay all bills promptly. I settle with judges, vets, caterers, etc., on the day of the ride. It helps toward reengaging them next year.

Catering

This has already been dealt with under Ride Hostess. Once this important aspect of the ride has been decided upon, it is best left entirely to the person willing to take it on.

Advertising

This should be done in advance but not too early, otherwise people tend to forget. I find that the best way is to place a brief ad early on in the local riding club or society's newsletter; then about a month before entries close, place another, more detailed, one. The local newspaper is also a good place to advertise and if a really large ride is planned, widely read magazines such as *Western Horseman* and *American Horseman* should be used. However, word of mouth and personal contact, as always, produce the best results. My experience has been that approaching local riders personally will double the entries over those obtainable purely from paid advertising.

The local press often shows interest in running a piece about the forthcoming ride, and they should definitely be contacted about doing a report (with pictures if possible) on the ride itself. The publicity will be useful for the following year's event.

The Ride Day

Most work has been completed by the actual day of the ride; now the main thing is to see that it all melds into a smooth-running operation.

With a heavy entry the day will start early so the whole ride does not drag on until dark. It is best for the first horse to be vetted thirty minutes before his start, so with a probable starting time of 8:30 for the first competitor, the various officials should be at ride base an hour earlier to set things up, meet incoming judges and vets, and introduce them to their recorders for the day. It is a help if each official has a badge with his name and job printed on it. It is also helpful if competitors can be advised of their starting time by mail as soon as the starting order is drawn up; their scheduled vetting time will be one half hour preceding their start time, and if they are ready for the vets 15 minutes earlier than vetting time, the vets can get going and, if possible, be a little ahead of their schedule, for no matter how smoothly the ride is run there will inevitably be hitches during the day.

Naturally the above applies to one-day rides, as the vetting for the two- and three-day events is done the day before ride start.

There should be at least three committee members on hand throughout the day to make decisions in case competitors query the rulings of the society or the decisions of the judges. This unfortunately does happen at times, even though ride rules state decisions of judges and vets are final. A committee must uphold these decisions or at subsequent events vets and judges will not be willing to assist.

Lists of all competitors should go to each ride official, judge, and steward.

Afterride Tidying Up

This consists mainly of seeing that the ride base is cleared completely of any ride traces and of picking up the markers. The Secretary should also write to the officials, thanking the judges, vets, farrier, police, first aid helpers, and so on, and in going over accounts make resolutions and notes for next year's event. Thank-you telephone calls to all club members who helped are an investment for future assistance.

Rides Available

FOR the benefit of those readers who are comparative new-comers to the sport of long-distance riding, I am listing here a selection of rides available in the United States. More experienced competitors will already know what is available, and the following notes are by no means a complete list, as this would be impossible with new rides coming into the equestrian calendar each year. Instead I have listed only the major ones, and readers will be able to find extra events by scanning various equine periodicals and, for local rides, by perusing their hometown paper. However, most rides are based on the rules and regulations of the accepted major fixtures, since ride organizers realize these Associations have a wealth of practical knowledge in this particular sphere.

First, it should be made clear that under the broad heading of "long-distance rides" there are three distinct categories, starting out with the pleasure rides. These are often one-day affairs but may be extended to five or six days, with mileage covered averaging about 20 miles a day. They are run purely for pleasure, all hint of competitiveness being absent, and they serve as an introduction to the upper echelons of the sport. Most riding clubs hold these events periodically.

Competitive trail rides vary in length from 25 miles in one day on up to 100 miles in three days. In these events there is an overall winner and often there are weight divisions. The main judging criteria relate to the condition of entrants over and at the end of the course, which is usually ridden at speeds of approximately 6 to 6½ mph. Timing only comes into the judging in that all mileage has to be accomplished within a generous time bracket. Horses outside this time bracket accumulate penalty points and if too far out are eliminated.

The final category is endurance riding, and here the winner is judged to be the first horse across the line provided, of course, he is sound. Here time is of paramount importance and there are no penalties for high speed, although at the other end of the scale no completion award will be given to any competitor who exceeds the stated time limit. This is usually 10 or 12 hours, depending on rules, for a 50-miler, and 24 hours for a 100-miler. This is total elapsed time, all veterinary stops being included in this estimate.

The main competitive trail rides run in the Eastern United States are listed below, together with their rule similarities and divergences. It will pay possible entrants to study all the rule sheets, as there are quite a few minor differences, and for those planning on a whole season these differences could be quite important in such matters as timing en route, division entered, awards given, equine health standards required, etc.

The seven major 100-mile-in-three-day competitive trail rides, together with the respective Secretary's address, are:

FLORIDA, Umatilla   Mid-March
      Sec. Mrs. Frances Threlkeld, P.O. Box 6225,
      Titusville, Fla. 32780
VIRGINIA, Hot Springs   Mid-April
      Sec. Mrs. William Hulbert,
      The Plains, Va. 22171
NEW JERSEY, The Wharton Tract   Late May
      (between Camden and Atlantic City)
      Sec. Mrs. Paul Adams,
      Medford, New Jersey 08055
NEW YORK, Skaneateles   Early July
      Sec. Dr. Robert Nichols, Gordon Street,
      Skaneateles, New York 13152
MAINE, Farmington   Early August
      Sec. Mrs. Connie Sween, North Highlands,
      Wilton, Maine 04294
VERMONT, South Woodstock   Late August

Sec. Green Mountain Horse Association,
South Woodstock, Vermont 05071
NORTH CAROLINA, Asheville   Mid-October
Sec. Mrs. William Cecil, P.O. Box 5375,
Asheville, North Carolina 28800

All the competitive trail rides have similar aims in that the rides exist mainly to demonstrate value of type, soundness, and selection of mounts for a long ride; to promote proper methods of care, training, and conditioning of entrants, and horsemanship and horsemastership among riders; and not least, to offer enjoyment to serious participants. These rides are very much owner/rider projects.

No artificial methods or stimulants are permitted on any of these rides. Horse boots, which means brushing and/or over-reach boots, are forbidden, as are bandages. All salves, liniments, and medications either external or internal are also forbidden. Water at ordinary temperatures only is permitted, ice to reduce fever being considered an artificial aid. Alcohol or salt on the back for toughening the skin is also banned.

Judging is done by a team of qualified personnel, sometimes three, sometimes two to a team, at least one of whom will be a veterinarian. The decision of the judges is final in all cases.

In addition to the team of judges there is a ride veterinarian on call throughout these rides. A qualified farrier is also on hand in case of need. All rides provide a stable manager to oversee the running of the ride base, and to ensure there are no rule infringements. There is also a night watchman who looks after the horses each night they are at ride base during the running of the event.

Timekeepers keep an accurate record of each entrant's time on course.

The course laid out is 100 miles in total, split into three legs of 40, 40, and 20 miles.

During the ride riders may not proceed dismounted, though they may rest their horses at any time they wish. Back at base all horses are permitted time to cool out, but once in their boxes may not leave them, except for the nightly veterinary chcck, until thcir numbers are called in the morning. No prior limbering up is permitted. Within certain time brackets, from the nightly veterinary check to stables opening in the morning, only the ride officials are permitted within stable area. All contestants successfully completing the course receive either a Completion Ribbon or a Completion Certificate. In some cases both are awarded.

Rides are open to stallions, mares, and geldings.

No blind horses may compete.

Next in order come the points in which most rides are identical but some differ slightly. Prospective participants would do well to acquaint themselves with these minor differences. (See pages 136–37.)

There are of course many other competitive trail rides and the main body concerned with these is the North American Trail Ride Conference, the NATRC, whose Headquarters address is 1995 Day Road, Gilroy, California 95020, and whose Secretary is Joan Throgmorton.

The NATRC aims and rules are similar in many respects to those for the Eastern 100-milers, but they have additional categories in which awards are presented as a matter of course. Judging is somewhat different in that it is split up into four categories as follows:

1. Soundness 40 percent.
2. Condition 40 percent.
3. Manners 15 percent.
4. Way of going 5 percent.

The NATRC provides two categories of ride. Class A rides are run over two days with 30–40 miles being traveled on each day over fairly level terrain. If terrain is precipitous or otherwise difficult, distances may be shortened to enable horses to finish within the allotted time of 6½ to 7 hours. Class B rides are one-day rides with mileage 30–40, and other aspects are the same as for Class A events.

The categories in which horses may enter are:

Open Division for horses five years of age and upward. The Open Division can be split into lightweight, heavyweight, and junior (ages 10 through 17). The Open Division Rides have

SPECIFICATIONS FOR

	Eligibility	*Medical Requirements*	*Scoring*
Florida	4 y. o. and over.	Health Cert. within 10 days of arrival. Negative Coggins Test within current year. Subject to Saliva and/or Urinalysis test.	100% Condition. ½ point per minute penalty under 6½ hours or over 7 hours (40 miles), 2¾–3 hours (20 miles).
Virginia	4 y. o. and over. 14 hands and over.	None spec. Supervision in stable.	Ditto.
New Jersey	4 y. o. and over.	New Jersey State health requirements and evidence of same. Recommend antitetanus shot. Subject to Saliva and/or Urinalysis test.	70% Condition. 30% time. 1 point time penalty for each 3 minutes outside perfect time score of 6½–7 hours (40 miles), 2¾–3 hours (20 miles).
New York	4 y. o. and over.	Negative Coggins test. Inoculations against communicable diseases advisable. Subject to Saliva and/or Urinalysis test. Nursing mares ineligible. Nerved horses ineligible. Horses blind in both eyes ineligible.	100% Condition. 1 point penalty per 3 minutes outside perfect time score of 6½–7 hours (40 miles), 2¾–3 hours (20 miles).
Maine	4 y. o. and over.	Health Statement current 30 days prior. VEE shot within past 3 years. Rabies shot advisable. Saliva and/or Urinalysis test may be given.	100% Condition. 1 point penalty for each 3 minutes outside perfect time score of 6½–7 hours (40 miles), 2¾–3 hours (20 miles).
Vermont	4 y. o. and over. Owner ridden (or whoever is competing from 1st August).	None spec.	80% Condition. 20% time. ⅓ point penalty per minute outside perfect time score of 6½–7 hours (40 miles), 2¾–3 hours (20 miles).
North Carolina	5 y. o. and over.	None spec., but subject to Saliva and/or Urinalysis test.	100% Condition. 1 point penalty per minute outside perfect time score of 6½–7 hours (40 miles), 2¾–3 hours (20 miles).

SEVEN EASTERN HUNDRED-MILERS

Divisions	*Awards*	*Stable Closing*	*Cooling Out*
Lightweight: 155–169 lb. Middleweight: 170–199 lb. Heavyweight: 200 lb and over. Junior. Catch weight. Ages 11–15 yr.	1st to 6th place for adults. 1st to 10th place for juniors.	9 P.M. to 5 A.M.	Not spec.
Lightweight: 120–160 lb. Middleweight: 161–200 lb. Heavyweight: Over 200 lb.	1st to 5th place.	9 P.M. to 6 A.M.	Not spec.
Lightweight: 155–180 lb. Heavyweight: 180 lb and over. Junior. Catch weight and ages 12–17 yr.	1st to 6th ribbons. 1st to 4th trophies.	9 P.M. to 5 A.M.	2 hours on 40-mile days. 1½ hours on 20-mile days.
Divided into light, medium, and heavyweight at weigh-in to distribute entries evenly.	Not spec.	9 P.M. to 5 A.M.	Not spec.
Divided into light, medium, and heavyweight at the weigh-in to distribute entries evenly. Juniors. Catch weight. Ages 11–17 yr.	1st to 6th place.	Stables shut after nightly vet. inspection.	Not spec.
Light, medium, heavyweight divided at weigh-in to distribute entries evenly. 140 lb minimum to be carried. Juniors. Catch weight. Ages 12–17 yr.	Not spec.	8 P.M. to 5 A.M.	Not spec.
Lightweight: 155–179 lb. Heavyweight: 180 lb and over. Over 235 lb at judges' discretion. Juniors. Catch weight. Ages 10–18 yr.	1st to 4th place.	9 P.M. to 5:30 A.M.	2 hours on 40-mile days. 1½ hours on 20-mile days. (Except at judges' discretion according to climatic conditions.)

Annual High Score awards and National Championships awarded at the end of each competitive season, plus a Sweepstakes Championship.

Novice Division for horses four years of age and upward. However, after a horse has accumulated 32 points in the Novice Division he must transfer to the Open Division. This rule does not apply to four-year-olds who, regardless of points gained, are still novices for that year. The Novice Division may also be split into lightweight, heavyweight, and junior (ages 10 through 17). Novice horses are not eligible for High Point and National Championship awards. Distance of rides for novice horses will be two thirds the distance of Open rides, or 20 miles, whichever is the shorter.

The weights to be carried in the lightweight and heavyweight divisions for both these categories will be: lightweight, 140 pounds up to but not including 190 pounds; and heavyweight, 190 pounds and over. The difference in sectioning these rides is that Open Division *will* have the subdivisions for weight carried, and Novice Division *may* have this division, at the ride management's discretion.

Although the main judging aspect of these rides is the evaluating of fit horses over a testing ride, horsemanship awards are also included in the judging so that competitors successfully completing the course may try for these in addition to the first through sixth place awarded on each ride. All NATRC rides have uniformity in judging in that each ride has the same divisions with the same weight to be carried in each, and the same number of awards in each division. Additional awards may be given if organizers so choose, but to obtain NATRC sanction their full set of rules must be adhered to. These rules are the same for each ride so that competitors know in advance what the judging criteria will be.

There are at present three regions sectioning the country, and the NATRC makes provision for adding to these regions as the need arises, and as the sport progresses.

The Regions are:

Region 1. Oregon, Washington, Idaho, and California north of Santa Barbara.

Region 2. Nevada, Arizona, and California south of and including Santa Barbara.

Region 3. Colorado, Wyoming, Utah, Montana, and New Mexico.

Each region has its own championships awarded on a points system, and there are also overall National Championships in the various categories, with the supreme award of a Sweepstakes Championship decided from the most successful entrants in lightweight, heavyweight, and junior divisions throughout the three regions.

Rides scheduled are too numerous to list, and their numbers are growing all the time, but full details on this important Society's events and schedules can be obtained from the Secretary, as mentioned earlier in the chapter.

The other side of the competitive coin is endurance riding; as already explained, this is the acme of the sport. In endurance riding a ride winner is determined by speed and condition in that the first horse across the finish line, provided he is sound and in a condition to go on, is the winner. Endurance rides are springing up all over the country and the main body governing these is the American Endurance Ride Conference, Inc. (P.O. Box 1605, Auburn, California 95603), which issues a very comprehensive list of events, and also has yearly championships in various categories, awarding trophies to horses of various breeds and individual horses who have accumulated a winning points tally throughout each competitive year. AERC rides are held in twenty states: Alabama, Arizona, Arkansas, California, Colorado, Idaho, Illinois, Iowa, Mississippi, Minnesota, Nevada, New Mexico, North Carolina, Ohio, Oregon, Texas, Utah, Washington, Wisconsin, Wyoming.

On the AERC schedule, the mileages tallied on rides give a breakdown in the following brackets:

Two rides of 25 miles each.
One ride of 26 miles.
Two rides of 30 miles each.
One ride of 40 miles.
One ride of 44 miles.
Forty rides of 50 miles each.

One ride of 54 miles.
Two rides of 60 miles each.
One ride of 75 miles.
Seven rides of 100 miles each.
One ride of 102 miles.

Other rides are being added as the sport becomes more popular.

The ride that takes pride of place as the pioneer of modern day endurance riding is the Tevis Cup, a 100-mile one-day ride held in late July or early August each year on a trail that begins in Squaw Valley and ends in Auburn. Run by the Western States Trail Ride, Inc., whose secretary is Drucilla Barner, the basic ride rules are as follows:

Riders must be a minimum of 12 years old, and juniors from 12 to 17 must be accompanied by an adult of 21 or over en route.

Horses must be serviceably sound and a minimum of five years old.

Horses competing for the two trophies, the Tevis Cup for the fastest time and the Haggin Cup for the horse in best condition from the first ten finishers, must carry a minimum of 165 pounds. Horses only competing for a Ride Completion Buckle may ride at weights lower than 165 pounds. No drugs or stimulants either orally or by injection are permitted, and feed and water may not be tubed.

Competitors are not eligible for any monetary awards.

Riders must follow the marked trail and be checked into and out of each checkpoint.

Successful entrants are those horses who pass a veterinary examination 45 minutes after finishing the course, and are then pronounced fit to proceed.

Throughout the ride there is strict veterinary control and three major mandatory stops of one hour each, during which time each horse is checked by the veterinary staff and has to be fit to proceed within the hour. In addition there are spot checks throughout the ride, a 30-minute check and two 15-minute checks en route, the latter two before the final climb into Auburn and at the outskirts of the city before going onto the finish line.

On the sketch map of mileage plus altitude in the ride literature, the major hourly stops are given as Robinson Flat at approximately 34 miles out, Michigan Bluff at approximately 61 miles out, and Echo Hills Ranch at approximately 85 miles out.

The route for this ride is both rough and tough, and over the past two decades the Tevis Cup has achieved worldwide renown, so that most other endurance rides run in the United States use the Tevis Cup format as a guideline. Other countries, including Britain for its first 100-miles-in-one-day ride in 1975, have drawn heavily on the tested format for running such an event, especially in the organizational setup, veterinary requirements, and ride rules, as models for their own competitions.

Full details of the Tevis Cup can be obtained from the Secretary, Western States Trail Ride, Inc., P.O. Box 1228, Auburn, California 95603.

From the brief notes on competitive trail and endurance riding events contained in this chapter, prospective competitors can make a start in planning their long-distance careers.

A Miscellany of Winners

THE foregoing pages have dealt with how to successfully choose, condition, and ride horses in competitive trail and endurance events. This final chapter introduces a few of the animals illustrated. Among these are members of my own family of endurance horses.

Nizzolan is a purebred Arabian stallion, bred in the United States but predominately of Crabbet blood. His sire, Lewisfield Nizzamo, was considered one of the best sons of the great Nizzam. Nizzam was bred by Lady Wentworth, exported to Holland, where he became a champion, and later taken to the United States, where he was also a champion and ranked among the nation's Top Ten. His dam, Solange, traces to Raktha, one of Britain's all-time great Arabians. Nizzolan himself, although a late maturer, has handsomely fulfilled the hopes I had of him when he was kept with endurance riding in mind, and the satisfaction is that much greater for having had him from the day of birth.

In his three years of competition in England he has won a Silver and two Golden Horseshoes, all with full veterinary marks; he has participated in five qualifying rides for the Golden Horseshoe (Britain's 75-mile endurance ride, run by the Arab Horse Society and British Horse Society), several pleasure rides, and also in all but one of the Endurance Horse and Pony Society Competitive Rides, three times gaining the award for the high-point Arabian awarded by the Arab Horse Society, and racking up enough points from rides successfully completed and rides in which he placed to stand Overall Grand Champion in the Manar Trophy for 1974.

In addition he has been shown successfully in dressage, ridden stallion, and riding horse classes under English tack. He has competed under Western saddle in pleasure, equitation, stock, trail, and versatility classes, and was 1973's and 1974's Reserve Champion Western Horse of Great Britain. He also goes happily under a sidesaddle, foxhunts regularly, and stands a full season at stud with a very high fertility rate, which I attribute mainly to the fact that he is kept extremely fit. When not working he runs at liberty with Katchina, a paint gelding, and his own son, Zoltan, a two-year-old colt. It is rare, at least in England, for a stallion to run at liberty but Nizzolan has an exceptionally gentle temperament which he passes on to his foals. On an ordinary hack Nizzolan often shows a lack of interest, as if to say, "Not this boring routine again," but immediately after he realizes he is on an endurance workout his whole attitude changes and he comes alive, digging in and moving effortlessly ahead.

Magnet Regent is a bay 15.2 ½-hand registered Standardbred mare I purchased as a long yearling before she went to the track as a trotter. Most of her long-distance work was done in the United States with the exception of a few qualifying rides in Great Britain and use as a back-up horse to Nizzolan in 1973. She successfully completed the Florida 100 Miler and the North Carolina 100 Miler at Asheville, where she was among the placing horses in what the judges termed a tough ride to judge as all the horses entered were so fit. In addition she competed on a local level in many long-distance rides, the most severe being a 56-mile race in 80-degree heat, which she completed in 4 hours, 46 minutes—9 minutes behind the winner. The winner went unsound as a result, while Magnet showed no aftereffects whatsoever. Her tremendous advantage is that being Standardbred she can really shift into top gear at an extended trot—the best endurance gait. Often out hunting I get amazed looks when she overtakes a galloping horse while still trotting comfortably within herself, as British-bred horses cannot approach the trotter's speed or length of stride. Contrary to what may be thought, this trot is supremely comfortable, even though it is coupled with an exceptionally powerful drive.

The mare's only fault, if such it could be termed, is that

she does not understand "enough." Like many horses bred to race, she has that inborn courage that does not know what quitting means. At 15 years of age she still has many years of hard work left in her, and after several foals by Nizzolan is going back into training.

Between them, Nizzolan and Magnet have produced what I hope is my future endurance mount in Zoltan, a rising 16-hand gray colt who seems to have inherited the best of both breeds: equable disposition, a really long stride, and very good bone. He will be brought out in 1978 as a five-year-old, and I could hazard a guess that he is the first horse in Britain to be bred specifically for this sport from stock proven on both sides to be suitable. However, with the sport's growth many people are now thinking of raising horses with this in view.

Katchina is a paint pony and the last of my current bunch. Bought as a three-year-old off the Gravesend salt marshes in Kent, he was about as wild as any pony could be; he had never been handled since birth and was more accustomed to seeing ships coming up the Thames Estuary than people around him.

Primarily intended as a riding-school pony, after settling and being broken, he proved above average in intelligence and generosity, which would have been wasted on a school pony. His combination of a very good stride and a competitive spirit led to his use as a back-up horse for endurance work in 1973, his five-year-old year (having a back-up horse prevents those last-minute disappointments should No. 1 go unsound at the last minute—a very real hazard in any equine sport, however much care is taken). With Nizzolan as No. 1, Katchina was piloted by three different riders in his first competitive year. He did two Qualifiers and the Golden Horseshoe Ride, in which he gained a Silver award, and the EHPS Devon ride (in which I rode him). At Devon he gained third place and high-point unregistered horse. Not bad for a 14.1 ½ pony of unknown breeding, and an encouragement to owners of the nonregistered horses.

Blue Peter is an eight-year-old crossbred New Forest/Welsh pony, blue roan, 12.2 hands high. He has made his mark very decidedly in competitive trail riding in England, being the smallest and also one of the most consistent little performers in

Hampshire. Always ridden by his equally diminutive rider, young Amanda Cox, he has competed in two Hampshire rides, first in a 40-miler where he was third, and next, in 1974, in a 50-miler, gaining a fitness score of 98 and first place over seasoned horses, many of which were Golden Horseshoe contestants. Blue Peter's toughness stems from the native pony blood, allied to which is the determination of his small rider, whose comment when asked if she could tackle long-distance riding was "If Peter can do it so can I."

Wendell T. Robie has been president of the Western States Trail Ride, Inc., for more than two decades, and has completed the 100 Miles One Day Ride thirteen times. Riding is only one of his many activities. In addition to being president of a large California bank and of a lumber company in his native Auburn, California, he is active in the world of skiing and is a member of the National Ski Hall of Fame.

He was seven years old when he bought his first horse—for twenty dollars, which he claims is the best investment he ever made. He happened upon some itinerant horse traders, and in talking with them indicated he would like to have a horse of his own, and that he had twenty dollars in savings at home. The traders were willing to sell a white mare for that price, and the deal was consummated. When Wendell's father came home that night, he insisted the mare be returned, and minutes later father, son, and mare were hurrying down the road, only to find that the horse traders had folded their tents and gone. A disciplinary thrashing was gladly endured, and on the white mare Minnehaha a famous riding career started. Wendell Robie has never been without a horse since that day.

It was perhaps thirty-five years later when he made another good buy—an Arabian yearling colt named Bandos. Bandos was the first horse to complete the Western States 100 Miles One Day Ride in 1955 at the age of fifteen. Again he finished first in 1956. His daughter, Molla, finished first in 1957 and 1958. Two sons and one daughter have won the Tevis Cup, and the Haggin Cup was won in 1965 by his son Siri. Probably thirty or more of Bandos's get have successfully completed the ride.

Not a typical Arabian breeder, Mr. Robie turned Bandos

out with the mares at his Pointed Rocks Ranch where feet and legs developed naturally for foals on the hard mountainous ground they traversed with such ease. Bandos was seldom shod and his get inherited his black hooves and his ability for traveling long distances as an ordinary day's work.

Today Wendell Robie rides Chapar, a grandson of Bandos through his granddam Hedia.

There can be very few riders who follow competitive trail riding who have not heard the name Lucille Kenyon, particularly those riders who compete on the East Coast circuit of 100-mile-in-three-days competitive trail rides. More specifically they will recognize her name when teamed with her champion Arabian gelding *Pazzam.*

It was back in 1951 that the long-distance riding bug bit Mrs. Kenyon, when she entered the first ever Florida 100 Miler on an American Saddlebred gelding named Truxton. Since that date she has entered every Florida 100, the only rider to do so, as well as all other major rides on the East Coast, and throughout the years has built up an enviable record of completion awards, placings, and an extremely impressive list of Champion and Reserve Champion awards.

Over the years 1951 to 1974 Lucille Kenyon has trained and ridden in competition a tremendous variety of horses of many types, both purebred and grade, including Saddlebred, Arab x Tennessee Walker, Morgan, Appaloosa, Quarterhorse, Arab x Quarterhorse, Quarterhorse x Thoroughbred, Standardbred, and Arabian.

It is with the last two breeds that she has achieved a major portion of her successes. She rode the Standardbred mare Beautiful Belle in six individual 100s for six outstanding achievements in the heavyweight division, winning first and Reserve Champion, 1959, Vermont 100; second, 1960, Florida 100; seventh, 1960, Virginia 100; first and Grand Champion, Florida, 1961; sixth, Virginia, 1961; and fifth, New Jersey, 1963.

The other even more remarkable partnership that still endures today is Lucille Kenyon and Pazzam, a rich bay gelding by the world-famous Nizzam out of Pamela. Now fourteen years of age, Pazzam has carried his owner through many thousands of training miles and, at this writing, over seventeen 100-mile trails in competition. In addition he has several times been ridden by other riders; under one of them he won in the Florida Junior Division in 1973. With Mrs. Kenyon he has racked up an impressive score of two completions, two sevenths, two eighths, one sixth, one fourth, two thirds, three seconds, and five first places. He has also been awarded the Reserve Championship three times and the Grand Championship four times—a tremendous record for a real partnership.

When it is considered that these 100s throughout the years were scheduled in different parts of the country, Pazzam's record is even more noteworthy. Starting with Florida's ride in March and finishing with North Carolina's in October, the climatic conditions range from extreme heat and humidity to cool sharp weather, with all the variations in between. Terrain varies even more greatly, from deep holding sand in Florida to mountains in Virginia with good footing to the constant hills of Vermont with their gravelly tracks to New Jersey's mixed going with some hard and some soft and heavy footing to Maine's stony tracks, Oklahoma's hard clay, and North Carolina's Smoky Mountain trails.

The success of this pair has been achieved the hard way, by an applied program well thought out, with no skimping en route —the only way to achieve continued success in competitive trail riding.

Since 1959, when Donna Fitzgerald first embarked on her chosen sport of long distance riding, her name has been synonymous with excellence. When partnered by any one of a succession of successful endurance horses, Mrs. Fitzgerald is a force to be reckoned with—and never more so than when riding her purebred Arabian gelding *Witezarif*. This pair has filled the winner's slot on the Tevis Cup four years in succession, as well as scoring wins and places in many other endurance rides, and awards for best-conditioned horse at the end of grueling contests.

The Donna Fitzgerald story goes back to when she was a teen-ager and, in her own words, "hung around a rental stable" —just as so many successful riders in various equestrian sports have begun. After exercising other riders' endurance horses, at sixteen she rode in her first Tevis Cup, completing only 85 miles, when both she and her horse were exhausted. This in no way weakened her determination to succeed (in fact, I think this determination to succeed, quite often deepened by a setback, is what characterizes endurance riders the world over) and the following year she did finish, taking the maximum time permitted and riding a quarterhorse mare. From then on there was no holding back, especially as in 1960 she met Pat Fitzgerald, already a confirmed enthusiast; in 1963, the year that he won the Tevis Cup on his Arabian gelding Ken, they were married and a formidable family partnership was formed.

From experience gained over the preceding few years and on a present from Pat, Donna made the big step from finisher to placer. She came in second in 1965 on the gelding Razlind, and went on to rack up many awards on this, her first Arabian. She reports that it was during this partnership that she learned one of her biggest lessons—that to be successful in endurance riding the competing rider must also be the training rider, for one of the few setbacks she received was when Razlind was conditioned by someone else and ridden by her in the 1966 Tevis Cup, which they failed to finish.

Realizing the toughness of the Arabian breed, the Fitzgeralds chose mounts of predominately Arabian breeding for future endurance competition. Their leading horses have been her husband's Anglo-Arab gelding Lanny, the purebred Ken, Preacher, and of course, Witezarif, who made his home with the Fitzgeralds in 1958. Witezarif has one of the most outstanding records for 100-milers of any horse foaled. He has completed seventeen 100 mile-in-one-day rides, no mean achievement in itself, but out of these he has won eight times and placed second six times. In addition he has several best-condition awards and also is a consistent winner and placer in 50-mile events.

It might be thought, as so often happens in the show jumping world where a rider has a once-in-a-lifetime horse which for a time wins everywhere and everything, that Witezarif is Donna's once-in-a-lifetime horse. He may be in her affections, but not in the performance rating in the Fitzgerald stable. Horses are Pat and Donna's livelihood and they have the material, the talent, and the dedication to take all the trouble needed to bring youngsters on and out into the endurance field. No chances are taken. Horses are chosen with endurance riding in mind, fed and conditioned accordingly, and given the commodity that so many horsemen in a hurry forget—time to mature both physically and mentally. Consequently the Fitzgeralds' mounts rarely place out of the top ten in any endurance ride. The facts speak for themselves: in 1971 on the Virginia City ride the first seven horses belonged to them, and in the 1974 ride the first four horses came from the Fitzgerald stable.

In addition to the husband and wife team, there are two additions to Fitzgerald riding power: young son Mike, who rode his first 100 when he was seven, and daughter Heidi, who at the age of six is tackling some of the 50-mile rides that are a fair task for older, seasoned riders.

Sorya, a black Thoroughbred mare, by the stallion Shapoor, foaled in 1959 and owned by the Matthew Mackay-Smiths, started her long-distance riding career by handily winning the lightweight division of North Carolina's Asheville 100 as an eight-year-old.

She was originally bought as a prospective broodmare for the Mackay-Smiths to put to their stallion, Old Fool, with the idea of raising potential endurance horses. Her broodmare days were postponed when the stallion died, and Sorya was entered at Asheville where she was ridden by an English girl, Elizabeth de Pelet. In previous chapters I have said that Thoroughbreds do not always make the best endurance horses and that their temperaments are not always suited to the stresses involved. Sorya is an exception, and her North Carolina win, in what the judges termed one of the most difficult 100s to judge in that all the entries were of such high caliber, paved the way for further expeditions. In the following spring she was sent to Colorado to go into training for the Governor's Cup. This is a 100-mile race run over two days with a 50-mile leg being ridden on each day, and the winning time computed on the two days' effort.

In this Matthew Mackay-Smith, D.V.M., rode Sorya, the pair achieving both a win and a new course record over tough ground in the Colorado Rocky Mountains with elevations up to 12,000 feet. Since then Sorya has reverted to the capacity for which she was originally intended, that of a broodmare. Her offspring, sired by an Arabian stallion, will no doubt be hitting the long-distance trails in coming years, for Anglo-Arabs often inherit the drive and toughness of the Arab and the added scope of the Thoroughbred.

Glossary

Diagonals. A normal horse (as opposed to a pacer, who trots laterally) trots diagonally, i.e., his near (left) fore and off (right) hind move forward at the same time, followed by his off fore and near hind. If the rider rises in the saddle at the moment the near fore is going forward, he is said to be on the left diagonal; if he rises as the off fore is going forward, he is on the right diagonal. The rider should alternate the diagonal he rises on so as to share the work load evenly; in this way the chances of one side of the horse stiffening are minimized. (You should also switch the side you rise to on a pacer.)

Impulsion. The means by which a horse moves forward correctly, using his hindquarters, for the forward thrust, thus lightening the forehand.

Leads. A horse is termed leading with the left fore when the left fore appears to extend first in the three-beat gait of canter (actually it is the right hind that is the leading leg in that that leg is the initial leg to strike into canter, but this is much more difficult to see). It is up to the rider to make sure the horse strikes off on the required leg. Alternating leads will share the work load and make for better balance.

On the Forehand. The way an unschooled horse travels going straight into the ground, lacking impulsion, in all probability leaning on the bit. A very tiring method of travel, putting undue stress on the forelimbs thus opening them up to more likelihood of breakdown in endurance work than those of the better-balanced horse moving with correct impulsion (or drive).

Rating. The means whereby the horse and rider progress forward at an even pace, not rushing one moment only to slow down the next. To rate a horse properly he must be sufficiently schooled to accept discipline, be prepared to move out or come down in speed as required. The rider must recognize at approximately what speed the horse is traveling.

Stabilization. Schooling the horse to such a standard that he will remain in a given speed and length of stride until the rider asks him to change it. Not as easy as it sounds; too many horses speed up as soon as rein pressure lessens, or the reverse—slow down as soon as the rider's legs quit pushing. Getting the horse to stabilize in his gaits is part of initial schooling.

HEALTH

Blistering. As applied to endurance riding can be a scalding where the horse's back temperature through airless tack contact heats up tremendously. Sudden exposure to cold air can cause hair to scald.

Colic. As applied to endurance riding can be caused by a number of reasons in addition to the normal ones:

1. Fatigue.
2. Too heavy an intake of water while hot or while excessively fatigued; by water too cold while body temperature remains high.
3. Too heavy a feed while fatigued. (Tired horses should be watered and fed sparingly and often, as a tired horse's digestion is not in its normal condition.)
4. Nerves. A horse that is excitably upset through different surroundings could colic, especially after extreme energy expenditure, if excitement remains unabated.

Cooling Out. The gradual process of lowering body temperature and getting muscles to unwind so no sudden changes take place. The best way of making sure the horse comes out limber next morning.

Dehydration. Loss of body fluids. Too drastic a loss can cause a horse to seize up. Guard against it by access to repeated *small amounts* of water throughout work.

Distress. The effects shown by the horse of being asked more than he is capable of producing. It will show most clearly in too high a heart rate, as well as unduly accelerated respiration rate. Mucous membrane will also be affected.

Fluid Balance. A horse needs to maintain enough fluids in his body to function adequately. As fluid is sweated out, body salts are also lost. Both must be adequately replaced, the fluid by frequent small amounts of water, thus preventing drastic loss, and the salts by addition to drinking water as needed.

Going Short. Shortening of stride through excessive fatigue and/or gradual stiffening through extreme exertion. Also can be indicative that a horse is "feeling his feet" or becoming sore.

Heart Rate. In a fit horse, 32 to 40 beats to the minute before exertion. Some horses' rates are slower, some faster. With hard work, rate approximately doubles but should decelerate rapidly when work ceases. If it doesn't, the horse is not fit, or alternatively may have some other irritant. If the horse is known to be fit, look for another cause, such as almost imperceptible lameness.

Mucous Membrane. This should be salmon pink in color. Deepening color to darker red shows fatigue. *Injected Mucous Membrane.* The darkened mucous membrane.

Pressure Bumps can be caused by ill-fitting tack. Also, some horses seem prone to them however many precautions are taken. Adequate padding and well-conditioned tack allied with gradual release of pressure over back area can help alleviate these.

Recovery. As applied to endurance riding, the speed with which a horse's heart and respiration rates approach normal after he has been subjected to the stress of hard work.

Respiration. In a fit horse this is between 12 and 18 to the minute at rest. Will approximately double after hard work, but will decrease rapidly when work ceases. Some very fit horses have a noticeably lower respiration rate both before and after work.

Scouring. Loose dunging. A sign of either excessive excitability or growing fatigue, or both. Constant scouring is very detrimental to maintaining a good fluid balance.

Stocking Up. Filling of legs around and just above fetlock area. If legs remain cool and swelling subsides after work commences, this, as with windgalls, should not cause undue concern.

Stress. A horse under pressure of sustained effort.

Thumping Respiration. Very visible hard contractions in respiration (hence the name) as opposed to normal breathing, or even breathing after exertion. The horse will be obviously distressed and in no state to go on. Also accompanied by injected mucous membrane. Caused from horse being overridden and not fit. A fit horse can cope with extra demands. An unfit horse cannot.

Windgalls. Swellings around fetlock area. Most horses who have been subjected to hard work have them. If they are soft and do not interfere with joint movement, and if swelling subsides soon after work commences, windgalls should not cause concern.

FEED

Carbohydrates. These provide the energy for sustained hard work.

Proteins. These act initially to form strong bones and tissues and in older, working horses to repair tissues.

Roughage. Fiber content of various feeds. A horse needs roughage to keep him in top shape internally.

TDN. Total digestible nutrients. Stated protein contents of various feedstuffs (grains and hays) are not the actual digestible percentage. This is usually about half of the stated figure and this difference should be taken into account when one is working out a horse's nutritional requirements.

Index